As Ever, Joe

Story of a Quiet Hero

Mary Jo Brill
and
Geri Magnuson

ISBN: 978-0-578-54066-5

Library of Congress Control Number:
2020906728

Dedication
In Loving Memory
of
Joseph H. Brill

This book is a tribute to Joe, and to all who serve.
We also dedicate it to the generations of Americans,
who like us, never knew that their loved ones were
true American heroes.

Authors' Note

In the writing of this book, we have made every effort to remain true to Joe's words. Only very minor edits have been made to his letters, such as the addition of commas.

Through a painstaking process, involving the use of calendars and multiple readings, we were able to place the letters in their current chronology. Despite the fact that this collection may be missing letters, is only one side of a correspondence, and was subject to delays in mail delivery, we are confident that these factors do not detract from the fidelity of the story.

Among the numerous sources we researched to support the timelines and narratives, there were some inconsistencies in the recounting of events and in the spelling of places. Although we are not historians, we believe we have presented the historical context with integrity.

Acknowledgements

Our sincere thanks to:

Marilyn Hammarstrom and the staff at The Fort Tuthill Military Museum, Flagstaff, Arizona. Thank you, Marilyn, for your support, and for accommodating Mary Jo on an off-season visit when the museum was closed. Thank you Andy Boyd for coming in and giving a private tour. Jim Warbasse, thank you for your knowledge and support.

Matthew Messbarger and the staff of Arizona State University Library, Phoenix, Arizona. Thanks, Matt, for putting up with Mary Jo and Geri for three days while they explored nine bankers' boxes of information.

A special thank you to Anita Szostak, for your great skill of photo enhancement.

A special shout out to The Tinley Park League of Aspiring Writers, especially Chris Drnaso, for their support and encouragement and for always believing we would get this done.

To our family and friends, who patiently waited for this project to be completed.

*"A day by day record of what's happened
to me these last three years would make
good material for a book."*

Joe
November 20, 1944

Uncle Joe

Joe was my uncle. He was also my godfather, in the true 1950's sense of the word. In those days, a godparent helped to raise you, acting as a second father, and loving you as one of his own. As kids, my sister and I spent a lot of time with our Uncle Joe and Aunt Helen, and our cousins Mary Jo and Linda. Uncle Joe created nicknames for all of us, which made us each feel special. Joe was the official chef and meat carver at our family dinners. He never looked happier than when he was serving the first slice of a roast to the family dog. Joe was a social man; he loved hosting an evening of playing cards or watching sports. He had a wry sense of humor and a jolly voice. Of all the things I miss about him, it's his voice I miss the most.

I got to hear that voice again, more than twenty-five years after Joe's death. My cousin Mary Jo invited me to join her in investigating some letters her dad had written during World War II. I was both honored and excited! For me, any project that involved hanging out with Mary Jo was a project for me, but to read actual letters from Joe was literally a gift from heaven.

When I went to Mary Jo's house for our first meeting, there was a small blue suitcase on the coffee table. Inside, there were disordered stacks of letters and black and white photos. They were dusty and smelled a little musty, but in pretty good condition for being almost seventy years old. Tossed into the pile, was an envelope from the War Department, awarding the Presidential Unit Citation to Joseph Brill. Uncle Joe a war hero? I had heard from my mother that Joe fought the Japanese in the jungles of The Philippines, but the realities of that had never really registered with me. Joe had never talked about the war; at least not to us girls. We hadn't heard any details. But come to think of it, I always felt safe and protected when Uncle Joe was around. Maybe hero wasn't so far-fetched after all. Perhaps these letters would tell the story that Joe never shared. It was time to meet the Joe we didn't know, the Joe from before our time.

Reverently, I picked up a letter. Would it be a love letter to Helen? Family legend said that Helen and Joe were pen pals during the war. But the salutation read "Hi Gang"; a letter written by a soldier to his friends back home in Chicago. Shakily, I began to read the letter aloud to Mary Jo. It was as if Joe had joined us in the room. How I had missed his voice in the years since his death! His sense of humor, his appreciation of the simple pleasures in life, and his way of making others feel special radiated from the page. Soon, Mary Jo and I were sobbing and laughing at the same time.

We made a date to meet again. Over the next several years, we got together regularly to work on what we now called "our book". Reading Joe's letters was like getting to know a younger version of the man we knew and loved. Through his letters, we journeyed with Joe through three and a half years of war.

Did Joe's letters describe bloody battles? Were they full of the details of jungle warfare?

Quite the contrary. With literary style, Joe wrote of his everyday experiences: the food, the entertainment, the trips to town, and most importantly the mail calls. He referred to the various battles as capers or problems. Despite his downplaying of the fighting, we could feel the physical and emotional toll the war was taking on him.

I realize now, after reading his letters, how much he wanted to get home to "put on carpet slippers" and enjoy civilian life once again. I believe that that is exactly what he did, but I also believe that he carried his war experiences with him for the rest of his life. He had seen enough death to appreciate that life is short and precious, and that life's little pleasures are what make it worth living. Through those years of sacrifice and deepening despair he clung to the joys of a swell song, a good film, a clever joke, or a few lines of news from friends back home. For the rest of his life, he never stopped appreciating those simple delights.

This project has been a true labor of love. During the years we have spent transforming Joe's words into this book, our own lives have progressed. We have had careers, celebrated weddings, mourned losses, and welcomed grandchildren. Life has kept us busy, but we never gave up on completing Joe's story. We hope you enjoy it.

Geri

Old Blue

The old blue suitcase was always there. Throughout my childhood and beyond, it remained. Sitting, unopposed on my parents' closet shelf, it held steadfast, holding an adventure inside, waiting patiently to be discovered.

I always knew the powder-blue, hard-shelled Samsonite suitcase was full of letters my dad had written during the war. I was never interested in reading them, but would go through the case from time to time to marvel at the photos he had taken and to read the captions on the back of them.

My dad passed away in 1987, but it wasn't until my mom passed away in 2008, when I was cleaning out her closet, that I became reacquainted with Old Blue. I'm ashamed to say that I had almost forgotten about it. Suddenly, that old blue suitcase full of letters became so important to me. It was that day that I realized it was more than a suitcase: it was treasure chest. All those years it silently held priceless treasure: my dad's voice...and a story beyond anything I could have known about my father.

As my cousin Geri and I started to put these letters in order, it became clear there was a story to be told. The more I learned, I was in awe of the 158th RCT, known as the Bushmasters, for what they endured. I am proud to say my dad was one of them. Their journey was long and extremely difficult, but all through it, they accomplished every objective they set out for. I also felt that this group was one of unsung heroes.

General Hanford MacNider was in command of the 158th RCT when they were in the Philippines, where some of their toughest fighting occurred. Perhaps he said it best when he said of the (unsung) 158th:

> "...No attempt has been made to recount the individual exploits of the dozens of units and thousands of heroic men who passed through this tough little command, (158th RCT), nor has any effort been put forth to picture the deadly heartbreaking monotony of life in the fetid dripping jungles of Panama, New Guinea, and its nearby islands, or the Philippines, where a combination of mountains and dense

tropical vegetation made a more difficult fighting country than any other south of the equator. Rain, heat, mud, fever, more rain- month after month, for many of these men year after year- bursts of fierce fighting, long dreary periods of continuous back-breaking labor- no furloughs, no diversions, no anything but more of the same. This constituted the life of the foot slogging Bushmasters."

General Hanford MacNider

Let the story begin...

Mary Jo

TABLE of CONTENTS

- *... but save this letter and someday I'll tell you all about it.*
- *... and first thing you know I was getting that homesick feeling.*
- *I understand there will be a leg show at the theatre.*
- *The floor show we were to have in the evening was called off because of.........I can't tell you, but we did see Abbott and Costello in "Rio Rita."*
- *The only way I have of knowing about the rationing and things that are happening at home are the letters I get.*
- *Come to find that I had malaria and before you could shake a stick, I was in the hospital.*
- *I'm getting a little restless of this hospital life and wish I would get returned to duty.*
- *If oranges and bananas were dollar bills we would all be millionaires.*
- *I don't think any more of walking twenty-five miles than I used to think of walking for a paper.*
- *That trip to Chicago for the holidays is one that this little GI wouldn't mind having a part of.*
- *...assuming of course that I do get back and those odds are dropping fast.*

Part III   Australia   Late January   1943
- *I'm in Australia and having the time of my not so young life.*

Part IV   New Guinea and New Britain   1943-1944
- *... came some more moving orders and I am now in New Guinea.*
- *... we had served our hitch in hell, but compared to this place it was a Sunday school picnic.*
- *A letter that contains news is just like listening to a radio or reading a newspaper.*
- *I think I could make a letter sound fairly interesting if it weren't for that censor man.*
- *....and take it from me, you do need a lift in this part of the world.*

- ...the best way of getting home in a hurry is to get this war won.
- One of the boys went out on a trek into the jungles yesterday and of all things-came back with a hog.
- Sure would like to trade some of this jungle fighting for some of that desert stuff.
- She told me of a dream she had recently in which I played the part of her third husband.
- I don't doubt that we will have our share of fireworks.
- Not even a bottle of beer.
- The holidays will be here again and me further than ever from home.
- What we need are playing cards for our bridge games. Yes, I said bridge.
- Getting back old and gray will be better than not getting back at all.
- In a short time it will be three Christmases away from home.
- I would like to see a few bright lights and hear some good music again.
- It looks like now that will have to wait for the duration.
- It's made from part of a shot down Jap Zero and the setting is part of a shell.
- I can remember when the mail calls were more regular.
- You guys are going to get plenty of first hand and plenty of bull...on how this war was won when we get back.
- Have been hearing some good things about the Bears.
- I polished up quite a bundle on the Yanks World Series victory.
- That White Christmas business does make a guy feel homesick for a few minutes.
- One of the boys used to make his living playing for Cab Calloway and another for Kate Waller.
- Think I'll put the letters off and try getting some shuteye before it gets too hot.
- Birthdays and holidays have all but lost their meaning to us.

- *...but you should see what goes on between these shows and these meals. Phooey on it!*
- *I would rather see a boat heading for the States, but that will come someday.*
- *... but I really have been unavailable.*
- *Think of me now and then and keep writing as often as you can even though you probably won't hear from me for the next couple of months.*
- *I'm ready to call it a day and come home for a while now.*
- *Things have been rather hectic for a while; I guess your newspapers have been having a field day.*
- *... the eternal tropical heat and equally eternal battle of the survival of the fittest.*
- *...phooey on this foxhole.*
- *Everything goes well during the day, but oh those lonely nights.*
- *I don't know how we got this far away from civilization, but we did.*
- *...showing the pictures you get from home is a ritual around here.*
- *...but I refuse to lose faith yet.*
- *It's funny how you can be smack in the middle of things, and yet know so little of what's happening.*
- *This is probably the only place in the world where a guy could lose that kind of dough and not feel bad about it.*
- *They are certainly doing their best to make up for the time we had to do without things.*
- *This sweating out that boat ride back to the States is about to get me down.*
- *No eggs, no bunny, no nothin'.*
- *... and life in these parts is too uncertain to pass up a little pleasure when you can get it.*

Part V   Dutch New Guinea   1944

- *"There are no atheists in a foxhole."*
- *… get in touch with the folks. They will be notified if anything happens to me.*
- *Finally had that bath and change of clothes.*
- *Had my first night's sleep above the ground the other night.*
- *…I've had my share of the fighting and would like to settle down with carpet slippers for a while.*
- *I'll never stop wanting to get back home, but I'm beginning to doubt if I will.*
- *Makes me suspect every time they start passing out fresh meat.*
- *… at long last the much- promised beer has arrived.*
- *We have been saving our rations and with luck we'll have six bottles per man.*
- *They don't want human beings in this army-what they want is a bunch of supermen.*
- *There doesn't seem a chance to get back before war's end.*
- *No doubt you heard about all the landings in the Philippines.*
- *A day by day record of what's happened to me these last three years would make good material for a book.*
- *… those damned tropical ulcers can be most annoying.*

Part VI   Philippine Islands   1945

- *We are geographically closer to home now than when we started, but as for getting back home…*
- *Happily, this last long break between letters wasn't occasioned by the doings of the Nips.*
- *…there is the much more important job of staying alive.*
- *Did I ever tell you that G Company was awarded the Presidential Citation?*
- *We're plucking up an occasional Nip or two now and then…*
- *Daddy doesn't live here anymore*

Prelude to War

World War II officially began in September 1939 when Britain and France declared war on Germany after Hitler invaded Poland. The United States claimed neutrality on entering the war, but helped the effort by supplying arms to Britain and France. When France fell in 1940, President Roosevelt pushed for military buildup. The United States also began to send ships, tanks and planes to the Allies. Knowing it was becoming more difficult to claim neutrality, President Roosevelt was preparing America for an inevitable war.

On September 16, 1940, the United States instituted the Selective Training and Service Act, which required men between the ages of 21 and 45 to register for the draft. This was the first peacetime draft in U.S. history.

December 7, 1941, "a date which will live in infamy," became the tipping point for America's stance on the war. In the early hours of a quiet Sunday morning, the Japanese attacked Pearl Harbor U.S. Naval Base. The goal of this attack was to eliminate the United States as a power in the Pacific. Japan had already taken control of Malaya, Singapore and the Dutch East Indies (modern day Indonesia). Without interference from the U.S., Hideki Tojo, General of the Japanese Imperial Army and Prime Minister of Japan felt he could achieve his ultimate goal: control of the eastern hemisphere. Tojo wasn't greedy; he was happy to let Hitler have the other half of the world.

President Roosevelt could no longer claim neutrality. The United States of America officially entered World War II.

PART I
NEW ORLEANS
December 1941

"Well guys, we have finally started on our way to hell knows where."

Timeline of the 158th 1940-1941

September 16, 1940
The Arizona National Guard is called into Federal Service after Franklin D. Roosevelt declares a national emergency. Under the command of Colonel Prugh Herndon, they join their parent organization, the 45th Division, at Fort Sill, Oklahoma. They train in combat and camp building for five months.

February 28, 1941
Well-trained men leave for Camp Barkley in Abilene, Texas. At this point in time, this move was the single largest move in military history. They will move camp many times over the next few years. Training in combat and camp building continues.

June 9, 1941
Joe is drafted into the army. He is sent to the 158th at Camp Barkley in Abilene, Texas. Joe receives almost six months of intense training for combat in the jungle prior to leaving the States.

December 7, 1941
The Japanese attack Pearl Harbor Naval Base. War is declared by President Roosevelt and Congress. Army orders detach the 158th Infantry from the 45th Infantry Division. They will now operate as a separate regiment. They prepare to leave Camp Barkley for an undisclosed location.

Christmas Day, 1941
The 158th eats their Christmas dinner on a train bound for New Orleans. This is the first leg of their very long journey.
The first letter of Joe's story begins the next day.

December 30, 1941
The 158th Infantry Regiment embarks from the Port of New Orleans toward the Panama Canal Zone as part of the Panama Mobile Force. Moving under secret orders, their job is to assist in guarding all aspects of the vital canal and to track down enemy nationals.

Friday, December 26, 1941
New Orleans
Dear John and Lou,

Sorry that I haven't been able to answer your letter any sooner, but I've been so damn busy every minute of the time since I received it. I'll even have to cut this answer short.

Well, guys. We have finally started on our way to hell knows where. We left Barkley at 4 o'clock Christmas Eve and rode the train all night and all Christmas Day until about eight-thirty last night. We are now in Jackson Barracks New Orleans waiting for our transports. Don't know just how long we will be here, but we will probably be gone by the time you get this letter. And I still don't know where the hell we are going to wind up. We had a complete physical examination with X-rays of the heart and lungs before we left Barkley. Also, had two shots for yellow fever so I guess it's the tropics. We are carrying two complete khaki uniforms in our packs so no doubt it will be warm.

I suppose you had a nice Christmas. I was feeling a little blue over the way things worked out over the holidays, but so were all the other boys so I can't complain too much. We had a turkey dinner on the train, but eating a Christmas dinner out of a mess kit is not so hot. The train stopped in a town called Lafayette, Louisiana about noon yesterday and we practically bought out a tavern. Managed to get beautifully plastered and that helped a bit. Then last night after we got settled down they told us there would be no pass as we might leave within an hour's time so four of us went over the fence and took off to see New Orleans. Believe me, it's a swell town. Didn't

3

get back until four this morning, but was still too drunk to care very much. But I'm paying the price today. We are unloading our equipment from the baggage cars and is it heavy. The battalion (which consists of about 900 men and officers) is hauling 1,000,000 rounds of ammunition and try and figure out the answer to that one.

Our mail is being censored so I will mail this through town and hope that you get it intact. However, when we get to our new home it will be tough letting you know exactly where I'm at, but I will try.

Time is getting short so I will close for now. I'll have plenty of time on the boat and will write more then. Say hello to all for me and thank Eleanore for the nice card she sent. Thank you for your card too. It had a beautiful sentiment.

Write soon and if you don't hear from me promptly it will be the delay in delivering your letter. It will go a long way to catch up with me.

As Ever,
Joe

PART II
Panama Canal Zone
and
Panama
1942

"Most of the country is jungle and it's plenty wild and wooly."

Although it was the bombing of Pearl Harbor that pushed the U.S. into World War II, FDR chose to send more power to the European Theatre, as Germany already controlled much of Europe. On December 8, 1941, the day immediately following the attack on Pearl Harbor, Japan invaded the Philippines. The Island of Luzon, where the Philippine capital Manila is located, was captured by Japan by December 22, 1941. Although General MacArthur and his troops hated to concede, FDR ordered them out of the Philippines by May 1942. Japan gained full control of the Philippines and her people. The famous quote: "I shall return" referred to MacArthur's promise to remove the Japanese and restore control of the Philippines to its people.

As the 158th began their journey, they were unaware of the role they would play in bringing MacArthur's words to life. But first, the Panama Canal Zone needed their protection.

Opened in 1914 by the United States, The Panama Canal created a shortcut between the Atlantic and Pacific Oceans. As a result, time and travel were tremendously reduced. During the war, protection of the Canal was essential to trade, economies, and the war effort. If the Japanese were able to capture the Canal, all sea transportation to the Pacific would have to go around South America.

Working as a part of the Panama Mobile Force, the 158th assisted in the outer defenses of the Canal. They patrolled the east coast of Panama, as well as the interior. Along with the canal, they guarded airfields and the Trans-Isthmian Highway. Their first encampment was at Chorrera, where they constructed their own camp.

The jungles of Panama were uncharted territory in 1942. The 158th had much more to do than guard the Canal. During their one-year stay in Panama, the Bushmasters built three camps. Machetes in hand, they cut down jungle to clear the land and carried lumber board by board through waist deep swamps. Their primary enemy was the venomous Bushmaster snake, who constantly made its presence known as they moved through thick jungle. Thus, they adopted the name Bushmasters along with the insignia of the snake and machete as their logo.

The Bushmasters Mobile Force Jungle School was the forerunner to the U.S. Army Jungle Operations Training. Their extensive training in jungle fighting caused General MacArthur to request that the Bushmasters be assigned to his command in the Pacific Theatre.

The Bushmasters experienced five phases of training. Phase 1 and 2 prepared them for enemy ambushes. Booby traps were covered in Phase 3. Stream crossing was covered in the 4th phase, where they learned how to cross streams and disappear into the jungle. Finally, the 5th phase taught camp building and bivouacs, which are improvised and temporary shelters that offer very little cover. Unfortunately, they learned that the best place to set these up was in the middle of a swamp or the densest part of the jungle.

The Bushmasters also had a hand in espionage while in Panama. They took part in hunting down enemy nationals who managed to locate themselves in strategic positions between the Atlantic and the Pacific. In one case, they discovered and destroyed a network of enemy short-wave radios.

Finally, they continued making themselves useful by testing clothing and equipment designed to combat the wet conditions that affected jungle soldiers and their artillery.

In addition, medications for parasitic diseases like malaria, and treatments for fungal infections also needed improvement. The U.S. still had a lot to learn about jungle warfare.

Sunday

Dear John and Lou,

Forgive me for neglecting you so long, but things have been so busy for me that I haven't had the time. No doubt you will have had a phone call from the folks telling you I would be a little late in writing by the time you receive this letter.

Our letter writing has been a little difficult since we got here due to a shortage of stamps and will probably stay that way until we get completely straightened out. We were only given twelve cents worth of stamps and since it costs us six cents airmail that is only enough for two letters. But no doubt by the time I receive your answer there will be plenty of stamps to be had and I will answer more promptly.

We haven't had a mail call for almost three weeks and I suppose there will be several letters from you in the pile when it finally gets here. I sure hope so as I am anxious to hear the news from home.

As you probably will have heard by the time you get this letter, I am now stationed here in the Panama Canal Zone. We left New Orleans a week ago last Tuesday and arrived here on Saturday. Since then it has been work, and more work getting the camp established and organized. As I write this, things are just about all in order and there is a little leisure time to be had.

Because of all the work there was to do I didn't have an opportunity to get around and see the country until yesterday. A party of us went out to do a little scouting yesterday and there certainly is a lot to be seen. Most of the country is jungle and it's plenty wild and wooly.

We have been restricted to our area while all the work had to be done so I haven't had an opportunity to get to Panama City which isn't too far away, but probably will get to go before I write again and will tell you all about it next time I write.

I suppose the weather back home is plenty cold by this time. I'm not trying to make you jealous or anything like that, but the temperature out here is about 80-85 degrees every day and the nights are just cool enough to be able to sleep well.

I had better close for now as we can only send about a half ounce for six cents and I don't have any more stamps. Say Hello to Joy and Janet, Tony and Laura, Brownie and Al for me, will you? And tell Frank and Kay that I will write them as soon as I can get some stamps. Say "Hello" to them too. And all the folks.

Write soon and send me all the latest news. I will probably have more to write about next time.

So until then,

As ever,

Joe

Sunday
Camp Chorrera after one month
Dear John and Lou,

Had just about given up expecting to hear from you when your letter finally arrived yesterday. In the last letter I had from home the folks told me they had called as I had asked them to do and that you had said you would write immediately. Well, to make a long story short, I waited and waited and finally took the pencil in hand and wrote you. Probably you will have received it by now. No doubt this letter I got was the one you told them you would write.

We finally received all the mail that had been sent to Barkley after we left and the mail that was sent to that New York address, but I was sort of disappointed to find there was no letter from you. Or possibly it still hasn't got here. At any rate, I was sure glad to hear from you again and now that we are more or less established, there probably won't be any more delays. Oh yes, speaking of delays, you sent your last letter airmail, but because of the fact that it weighed more than a half ounce it was sent by boat thereby taking eight days to get here. By air mail it takes only from two to three days. So watch that in the future, will you?

Well, guys, day by day in every way I'm getting more sold on Panama. I guess it is only natural to resent a place so far from home, but this country and the people sure do grow on a person. Every time I get a letter from home telling me how cold it is there I think a little more of this place. We've been here exactly one month and most of the boys are looking like natives. I guess after a year or two of this our skin will be dark forever and a day.

10

I just got back Thursday from an eight-day trip to another camp for some combat work and field firing. This camp was located near an air base and we had the opportunity to go and see a few movies. (the first I've seen since leaving the States) and it was rather nice. In fact, everything about that camp was nice with the exception that it was set on sandy ground and the ocean breezes made a sort of a miniature dust bowl most of the time. Upon getting back here to Chorrera we found they had built an open-air theater here in camp. Now we can go to a show every night of the week. That sure will help pass the time away.

I still haven't had a chance to go to Panama City as yet. From all I hear I haven't missed anything, but I'll have to go and look for myself one of these days. Will write about it after I've been there.

Before I forget, the folks told me they had a registered letter for Brownie. From the way they write they seem to think he has gone home with his folks. Tell John to figure out some way for him to get that letter.

I wasn't too surprised to hear that Brownie has been classed 1-A. Too bad he didn't go into the service when I did. He would be well-trained and better able to take care of himself now. Have John and Frank heard anything from their boards lately? How does it look for them?

I was surprised to hear about Joy though. Has he been hitting the liquor as hard as all that? Sounds as though he's going rum-dum.* I'll bet he felt pretty bad when he sobered up and heard what he had done. I can well imagine how Janet felt. Be a long time before he hears the end of it.

11

I was glad to hear that you had such a nice Christmas. As you know, I spent Christmas on the train and New Years on the boat so I haven't much to crow about. The folks wrote they had bought me two defense bonds for a present, but forgot to tell me how much they are worth.

Had a letter from Virginia* last week and she told me all about the Sonja Henie Ice Review. I bet it was swell.

Guess I'll have to close before I exceed the half ounce so until I hear from you (soon I hope).

As ever,
Joe

Say "Hello" to Tony and Laura, Joy and Janet, all your folks and everyone else and don't forget to write soon.

*rum-dum - pertaining to, characteristic of, or arising from habitual drunkenness; addled by drink (dictionary.com)

*Virginia is Joe's sister

Sunday

Dear John and Lou,

Seems like somebody is always apologizing for not writing sooner, but I really haven't had a chance to write before now.

We were out on a scouting and patrolling party in the jungles these last three days and it was next to impossible to do any writing out there so I decided to wait until I got back before writing.

Had a nice trip through some of the wildest country in the world. While we were out there a party of six of us went across the mountains. We packed our food and were gone from our base camp for two days. We went across the Continental Divide and back again. And take it from me, it is one of the roughest and toughest trips I ever hope to make. It did me a lot of good though. I had been laying around camp for a couple of weeks and I was starting to get soft, but that kind of work would put muscles on a glass of milk.

I got back to camp here in Chorrera to find most of that long-lost Christmas mail had finally got here. Among others I found your letter dated the 30th of December.

I was glad to hear that you had such a swell Christmas this year. (or should I say last year). As you know, we didn't have much of a Christmas and I'm glad to know somebody had a good time.

Had a pleasant surprise in the form of a package from Verla. It contained a rather nice shaving set, (shaving cream, blades, after shave lotion and talcum) some candy, gum, and cigarettes and also a box of cookies which were too far gone to be saved because of the long time the package took in getting here.

13

Also had a letter from home telling me they had a very nice Christmas and that I am now the owner of two defense bonds. They will come in handy when I get out of the army. Looks like all of John's competition left when I came into the army. Isn't there anyone else around who can take his measure in a pinochle game? I can just see him sitting around and gloating while the rest of the club sits with baited breath waiting for his majesty to decide where he is going to go.

What's the latest on Brownie? Has he been told to report yet? And what about you John? Have you heard anything from your board lately? Or Frank? Do you suppose they will reclassify you soon?

We hear very little news of what's happening in the States out here beyond the little we get in the mail. But I suppose there have been a lot of changes since I was home last. Have they tried any blackouts in Chicago yet?*

I finally took that much-delayed trip to Panama City yesterday. The boys had already told me that it was nothing to write home about, so I wasn't disappointed at what I saw. It's a big enough place, but for the few places where the white people live (and there's not too many of them). It is all native in people and customs. There are plenty of honkey-tonks and liquor is dirt cheap (as are the women), but beyond that there is nothing. That one trip is enough to last me another two months.

Has Frank finished his model plane yet? That guy finds the craziest amusements. And how is the weather behaving? Still hot as blazes out here. It won't be too long before spring sets in back home. How does the work situation look for the spring season? Do you think there will be as much as usual?

Well, I'll be running out of space before long so I will start to close for now. Say hello to all your folks, to Joy and Janet, Tony and Laura, and Frank and Kay. Speaking of Frank and Kay, why don't they drop a line now and then. I would sure like to hear from old Baldy.*

Will say "Goodbye" for now, don't forget to write soon.

As ever,
Joe

How is Joy behaving after that splurge?

*Blackout rules were intended to make it difficult for enemy planes to see their target. Blackouts were a regular occurrence on the west coast, as it was assumed Japan would strike from the east. Despite Chicago's Midwest location, Chicago conducted mock bombing and air raid siren tests. In mid-1942, Chicago conducted two city-wide blackouts.

*Baldy is Joe's nickname for Frank

Thursday

Dear John and Lou,

I was just a little surprised to get your letter. I had written you only the day before and wasn't expecting to hear from you for at least a week. Ever since all that Christmas mail got in I've been on a merry go round trying to get letters straightened out and answered until I don't know from nothing any more. I guess it's about all here now though and maybe I can get back to normal again.

Well, how is everything going back home? Is the weather still cold and snowy? I was glancing through an old newspaper the other day and I was surprised to see that the major league teams were all set to leave for spring training. The weather being what it is down here almost made me forget that spring is just around the corner in the States.

So Brownie is just about in the army eh! How does he feel about it now? Is he still all hopped up about the idea? If you should see him, I wish you would give him my address and tell him to write and tell me all about it. I don't know his address so can't very well write to him.

Life has been softer than a feather bed these last three days. The company has been out on outpost guard these last three days and won't be back until sometime tomorrow. The few of us that stayed behind have been living the life of Riley. But all that will be changed next Monday when we are supposed to go out for two weeks of maneuvering with another outfit. Will write more about it when I get back and think nothing of it if I'm a little late in writing as I may not have the time or place to do anything while in the field.

As you know, we have an open-air theatre here in camp now. The sound and vision is good but the pictures are not exactly the latest. Can't complain though as even old pictures are better than no pictures at all. Have also been devoting some time to learning how to speak Spanish. If we stay here for a year or two I'll be a regular Spaniard when I get back.

That's about all I will have time for now so I will close. Say "Hello" to everyone for me and don't forget to write soon.

As Ever,
Joe

Did you ask Baldy to drop a line?
That's quite an epidemic of babies you guys are having in Chicago. Everybody doing their part for the army, eh! Too bad about Al and Ruby. I hope there is nothing wrong with their baby. They do have a lot of bad luck, don't they?

Joe

Monday, am
Dear John and Lou,

Came back from maneuvers on Saturday morning and found your ever-welcome letter waiting for me. Since you said you would like a few more details about Panama City and since I was expecting to go in yesterday I decided to wait until today before writing and give you a few more details.

Of all the things in the world you might know I would find a racetrack. Believe it or not they do have a pretty decent track where they have eleven races every Sunday. It's not a bad looking place. They have a six-furlong track and a big grandstand. The whole shebang is about the size of Sportsman's Park.* But the horses. What a difference. They run a mile and an eighth in 1.60 which as you can see wouldn't be worth a damn in the States. But fortunately, all the plugs are in the same class so it goes to make some pretty close races. I was splitting two-dollar bets with one of the boys and we won $19.60 between the two of us.

Incidentally, the track is in a section of the city that I had never seen before and I guess I'll have to take back what I said about Panama City being nothing to write home about. This particular section is very modern and up to date and it sure was a surprise to me. But I still can't say anything nice about the rest of the town.

Well, I could tell you about the maneuver we were on last week, but I know most of it will be censored so I won't waste the paper and ink. We left here last Monday and were gone six days, getting back here last Saturday. It was rough and tough all the way and everybody was glad to get back.

I do have a little news I think will get past the censor, though. We are going to move out of this camp sometime next week. We are going to a fort on the Atlantic side of the canal. I hear they have barracks there so it will be pretty good for us I reckon. Will write more about that later, but in the meantime, you can continue to write to this address.

I suppose by the time you get this letter Brownie will be in uniform. How did he feel about going into the army? Be sure to write me all about where he is and what he's doing. That is of course, providing he writes and tells you. I guess if there's anyone worse at writing letters than Baldy, it must be Brown.

Don't forget to let me know how your reclassification comes along, John.
I guess the army will have to be in a bad way before they start to take all of you old boys into uniform.

It does seem strange that you should get your new papers before Frank. How does Baldy feel about the whole thing? Looks like a good bet that he will wind up in uniform when he gets reclassified.

How is everything going back home? Are you still having a lot of snow and cold weather? I'll bet you are glad spring is just around the corner. It's probably getting dull to read, but the weather is still perfect out here.

What's that about Joy in an accident? When the hell is he going to learn that he can't hold his liquor? He had better quit before he gets himself killed.

Well, I see that I'm about to run out of space so I will start to close. I'm feeling like a million and am hoping this letter finds all of you the same. Say "Hello" to everyone for me and don't forget to write soon.

As Ever,
Joe

* Sportsman's Park was a horse racing track located in Cicero IL. It opened in the 1920's as a dog racing track, with Al Capone as one of the owners. In the 1930's it was converted to horse racing. For over 70 years, Sportsman's Park delivered horse racing entertainment to Chicago land until it closed in 2002. The town of Cicero purchased the land in 2003, and in 2009 it was demolished for urban development.

Monday

Dear John and Lou,

I've got the strongest hunch that I'm going to get a letter from you in this afternoon's mail. In fact, the hunch is so strong that I'm going to start answering now. Seriously tho, this place we are in now is the toughest place for writing you ever saw so I'm going to make the most of the few moments I've got. I may not get another chance for the next three or four days. Your letter is way overdue. I'm expecting it this afternoon.

I had a letter from home yesterday and the folks told me that you were over at the house, John. So, Brownie is finally in the army. I understand that you had quite a time with him the night before he was inducted.

Come to think of it, there's no use in my asking you a lot of questions. The answer may be in your letter when it gets here.

Maybe I will talk about a few things that are news in the meantime. For instance, we are now in a new home. We left Chorrera last Saturday and came down here to Fort Davis on the Atlantic side of the canal. Let me tell you, it's the answer to every soldier's dream. Big beautiful barracks with all the trimmings including hot water. You have to bathe in cold water for over two months to appreciate hot water. It sure is nice. We also have outdoor swimming pools and of all things, a golf course.

We were only there two days before they sent us out on outpost duty for ten days so I never had much of a chance to get around and see things, but I'll make up for it when we get back and write more about it then.

21

But it is the nicest thing that happened to me in the army as yet.

Right now, we are in the middle of the jungle again on outpost duty. It's pretty dull and we are looking forward to when we go back to Davis.

Hold on to your seat. I am planning and scheming to get into the Air Corps. I haven't done a thing about it yet except think about it but I am going to get all the details and see if I can manage it. Course I don't know if I can pass the exams but there is no harm in trying.

I guess I will stop for now and wait for your letter.

Well, at long last your letter got here. Good things come in bunches. There were two of them. One was dated February 27th and the other March 3rd. Both of them have been pushed all over the regiment due to the fact you make the G in the address look like an A, Lou.

It was sure nice hearing from you again. It's surprising how I miss your letter when it's a few days late.

So, Brownie was sent to Camp Grant for a while. He had better luck than I did when I was there. You remember I didn't stay there long enough to get into Chicago for a weekend. Wouldn't it be strange if he were to be sent to Camp Wolters? I wouldn't be too surprised.

So, you have a bone to pick with me, eh. Well, I hate to let you down Lou, but as a matter of fact I never received any Valentine Cards from you or your mother. I don't have any idea what could have become of them. They must have been lost on the way or something. Where did you address it to?

You've got me all on edge waiting for your next letter and the <u>real</u> news you spoke of.

I certainly would like to see John and your father together, Suzy.* I know how you must feel about it. Even way out here in Panama I find it hard to believe. But it should have been that way right from the beginning. Have you had Eleanore's opinion yet? Knowing Eleanore, I don't suppose she has much to say either way.

Speaking of Eleanore, I wish you would send me her address. I would like to drop her a line.

I just read your letter thru again trying to get an inkling of that real news you spoke of. It wouldn't have anything to do with John's dads' new love would it? Does it look like wedding bells?

Baldy has gone back to his old tricks again. I wrote him about a month ago and still no answer. Ask him how come, will you?

Sorry to hear that Grandma is not feeling so well. Give her my best and tell her I am looking forward to a hot game of cards in the near future. Well, maybe not the near future but some day not too far off.

I guess I will stop writing for now or I will be over the limit again. Say "Hello" to Tony and Laura, Frank and Kay, your family and Joy and Janet and don't keep me waiting too long for that real news. Keep me posted on the doings of Brownie.

As ever,
Joe

*Suzy is a nickname for Lou.

... to move in with Frank and Kay. But it's a good idea I think. What is John and Frank's dad going to do? Will he continue to live at Kimball? Seems to me it will be pretty big for just the two of them. And what about Millie? Will she live at Kimball or on Dickens?

From the sound of your letter there must be an awful lot of moving going on this year.

Frank's letter had quite a bit of news about Brownie. He gave me all the latest on the guy including his address. I wrote him a letter yesterday afternoon and I hope to hear from him soon. But knowing Brownie I won't be too surprised not to get a letter.

I don't think I will have the time to finish this letter this morning. It's just about time to eat and there are four of us who plan to go out and play some golf this afternoon. So I will stop for the time being and finish when I get back.

Well, here I am back again. Just got in from a rough and tough eighteen holes of golf and believe it or not I succeeded in breaking a hundred. I don't know what came over me but I couldn't do anything wrong today. I even managed to start and finish with the same ball. The first time in my brilliant golf career have I ever done that. I think I will send along the score card. It's surprising what a fine golf course they have put here on the post. As you can see by the score card it is fairly long and it has all the jungles, hills, and creeks you could want. I only hope we stay here long enough to give me a few more cracks at it. And the nice part of it is, they give you a bag of clubs and there are no green fees. All it costs is the golf balls which you have to furnish yourself. Not bad, eh!

I'm pretty sure we will be going out into the jungles on outpost duty again in a few days or so. Don't know where and couldn't tell you if I did, but no doubt our mail will come through with the supplies as usual.

I wish my Spanish was at the point where I could start teaching it by mail. It's taking me a long time to get to understand it and I doubt if I'll ever be able to write it. Fact is, I never expect to. But if you really care about learning to speak it there is a book (<u>Hugo's Simplified Spanish</u>) that is cheap and easily understood. But I warn you if you don't have people around who can speak it it's a tough job.*

I have applied for a permit to take pictures around the post and I hope to be able to start one of these days soon. I'll send you a flock of them. One of these days you can start an album. How does that sound? If I keep them around me they will just get ruined.

I still haven't been to Colon yet. Don't know what's the matter with me. I've got the money to go, too.

Well. It's getting late so I will start to close for now. Say "Hello" to everyone for me, will you. And write soon.

> So long for now,
> As ever,
> Joe

*I was tickled to hear that Uncle Joe was studying Spanish. I never knew that about him, and I became a Spanish teacher. I sure wish I could talk to him about that.
Geri

Wednesday

Dear John and Lou,

Received your very interesting letter just a few moments ago and as I am sitting here suffering all by myself I think I will start to answer now. It might ease the pain.

I just got back from the dentist a few hours ago and I am reminded constantly that I just had a tooth pulled. (I mean the pain constantly reminds me.) One of my pet cavities will no longer take half of my meals away from my stomach.

It all started about two weeks ago when we had a dental inspection. I was told then the tooth was bad. (I knew it all the time) but as it has never given me any trouble I just forgot about it. Then yesterday afternoon I was told that I would have to go to the dentist this morning. The doctor looked at it again and he told me that even though it was not giving me any pain now it probably would in the near future and when that time came I might not have a dentist so near at home. Well, to make a long story short, he finally talked me into having it pulled. The stuff he shot into my gums is just starting to wear off and I can feel it.

The rest of my company is in the field and I'm just shuffling around waiting for that tooth to stop aching. That is, I was just shuffling around until I got your letter. Now I'm scribbling around.

Lordy, Lou, from the way you started that letter I just couldn't resist reading it from the last page to the first. (just like a murder mystery story) to see what all that good news was about. At first, I thought John had been drafted or something. I couldn't imagine anything else that would make you so happy.

Seriously tho, knowing how that matter always was in your mind, I can see why now that it's finally straightened out you are up in the clouds.

What's come over the old man? Is he going soft? And why does everybody always give in to John right or wrong. I can just see the heel sitting back and looking smug with that I told you so expression of his. There will come a day. I'm glad for you that it's all finally worked itself out.

I wrote you a letter just the other day. I don't see how you could have gotten it so soon or did you just write on the spur of the moment? If so, I hope you have a lot of moments, because it's always nice to hear from you.

No doubt by the time you have received this letter you will have heard from Brownie. Where he was sent and what he's doing. Be sure to tell me all about it as I don't have much faith in his writing to me. He'll probably lose my address or something.

I had that letter you spoke of from Frank and I answered it over a week ago. I suppose he'll put his airplanes away one of these days and answer it.

I have a little news for you, but it will have to wait until the next letter as I can't write about it until after it happens. It won't be too important but what it won't keep for another week or so.

The folks told me last letter that John had stopped in for a bit last week. Did they say anything about Evelyn to him? You know, the lawyer sent me some legal papers to sign and I guess by now I am pretty close to being a free man again. It will be best that way.*

I keep writing and that damn hole in my mouth keeps aching. It looks like the hole is going to win.

27

I'm just about out of news, so I will close for now and see if I can scare up some warm salt water and gargle a bit. Say "Hello" to all for me and don't forget to write soon.

As Ever,

Joe

I suggest you buy <u>Twenty Easy Lessons In Spanish,</u> and get busy or you will never catch up with me.

J

*The mention of Evelyn and a divorce was a little shocking. For most of my life I had no idea Uncle Joe had been married before. It was always Uncle Joe and Aunt Helen, my father's sister. It was at the luncheon after Joe's funeral and after more than a few cocktails that Auntie Helen confided to me that Uncle Joe had been married before. Without missing a beat, I said "before the war?" Helen said "yes" and the conversation flowed on to other topics. I never brought it up to Mary Jo; I wasn't sure if she knew.
Geri

* I remember once hearing something about his "first wife" as a child, so somewhere in the back of my mind I knew.
Mary Jo

28

Monday am

Dear John and Lou,

Received your swell letter yesterday and I don't have to tell you how good it was hearing from you. I really didn't expect to get another letter in so short a time, but don't get the idea that you're writing too often. I would like to hear from you guys every day, but the way you cover the news when you do write, well! You probably wouldn't be able to say more than hello and goodbye writing every day.

I still haven't heard from Brownie as yet, but it's only been a week since I wrote him so it will be a few days yet before his letter gets here.

Just about time to be hearing from Baldy too—that is; if he don't decide to wait a month or two to "let the news pile up" as he puts it.

There's no use in my asking how is everything going for you. Your letter makes it sound pretty good.

As for me, everything is still going along perfectly. There are still no signs of our leaving (censored) and no one is looking forward to leaving. I'm so caught up with playing golf and swimming that I'm passing up the chance to go today. I've been out almost every day this week and it sure has been swell.

But I suppose like all good things it will come to an end one of these days soon. Then back out in the jungle we go.

Went to the show the other night and saw Walt Disney's "Fantasia."* I'm not sure, but I think the army has taken away my love for the finer things, because I walked out in the middle of the thing. It was certainly a pain in the neck to me. I just ran out of ink, so had to borrow another pen to finish this letter. Plenty of variety, both red and green ink in one letter. Anyway -

Last night they had Edward G. Robinson in "The Unholy Partners" and it was a lot better. I expect to see "Rise and Shine" this week. It looks pretty good.

Tomorrow is payday and everyone is looking forward to going to town and making a little glad. I still haven't been to Colon, but will break down and go sometime this week.

No doubt you have read in the papers about Congress passing a bill that will give the boys in Foreign Service a twenty percent increase in pay.

I guess we will get over four months back pay in our next month paycheck and it won't be hard to take.

Seems hard to realize, but it's been almost a year now that I'm in the army. Time certainly does fly.

I've sent home for my birth certificate and when it gets here I'm going to make another attempt at the Air Corps. One of the boys in another company made the grade the other day, so at least I know it can be done. No harm in trying.

Glad to hear that your grandmother is well again, Lou. Say "Hello" to her for me and tell her that card game is a date.

How is everything coming along with your moving plans? Have the boys started to get very busy yet? Had a letter from home the other day and the big fellow* is in a sweat about having to clean up the two flats on Avondale and Farragut by himself. Believe me, this is one time I would welcome working there on a Saturday and Sunday.

How are the newlyweds getting along? I'll bet the old man is having the time of his life. Say "Hello" to them for me.

Well, it's getting time to go out and get busy so I will close for now. Say "Hello" to all for me and write soon.

As ever,

Joe

P.S. The tooth that isn't there is giving me no trouble at all! I hear you're enjoying some honest to goodness spring weather these days. The weather is still as nice as ever out here, but the rainy season is not too far off and when it comes, who can tell?   Joe

*I was surprised my dad hated "Fantasia", because he loved both music and animation. Mary Jo
*The "big fellow" remains a mystery. As the story progresses, it becomes more apparent to me that he was a member of my grandparents' household. Mary Jo

31

Wednesday pm

Dear John and Lou,

Received your letter at long last. I was beginning to wonder what had happened to you; I hadn't had a letter in such a long time. It never occurred to me that with all the usual work plus all the trouble that goes with moving you might be too busy to write. I'll bet you will be glad when it's all over and you're settled down again. Too bad about the people refusing to vacate. What is there you can do about it? I suppose just sit back and wait for them to get out.

The boys certainly aren't wasting any time going fishing this year. How in the hell can they find time to go two hundred miles in the middle of the rush?

I'm still waiting to hear from Brownie. What did he have to say? I guess you might as well write me about it as he probably won't write for another month or two.

I've had time to write Eleanore, but I don't have her address. I've looked all through my locker for the letter you wrote with her address and can't find it anywhere. I must have thrown it away or something. So if you haven't told her to write me as yet- send me her address again and I'll write her.

Before I forget- we've got a new address again. The new one is :
PvT Joe Brill
Co G 158th INF
Fort Clayton, Canal Zone.

We spent a few busy days last week, but things are back to normal again and no complaints.

I got a pass and went to Panama City last Sunday - the first trip to town in almost two months. Where did I go? I went to the races. Had a good time and even managed to win a few dollars. We took some pictures at the track and as soon as they are developed I'll send you some. Speaking of pictures- I still haven't got the others out yet. It's plenty hard to get around some times. I'll send them as soon as I can. We went into the city after the races and had a few drinks. I didn't get drunk, but even so I felt like a wreck the next day. I can't stay up after eleven any more it seems.

The biggest topic of conversation around camp these days is our next payday period. We will get that twenty percent raise for Foreign Service and since it will be paid from the first of the year it will make a tidy sum.

I have managed to keep up with baseball fairly well. The Panama paper has the scores printed every day and we keep up on things. Looks like the Cubs are playing a little over their heads doesn't it? One of these days the Sox will start winning those games they have been losing by one run and then watch them go.

Well, I wanted to write you a little about some of my friends in the army, but I'm just about out of time so I'll save it for next time. Say "Hello" to all for me and write soon.

As ever,
Joe

Weather and health are still perfect. Did you ask Baldy to write? Now that he's been fishing I suppose he has enough to write about and I'll probably hear from him soon.   J

Wednesday, the 15th
Dear John and Lou,

Got your swell letter yesterday, but was too busy to do anything about answering until this morning. That was the shortest letter I can recall ever getting from you. When I opened it and found only two pages, I tore the envelope to pieces looking for about three or four more sheets. Either you were pressed for time or there is a dearth of news to write about. I imagine though that you are being kept plenty busy getting ready to move.

It was news to me that John and Frank have been doing some work for the folks. I'm expecting a letter from home today and no doubt there will be something in it. Speaking of work- how is everything going for the boys? Plenty busy by now I'll bet. It sure would be nice to get in on some of it.

That must be quite a place you dined at out in Hinsdale. Still nothing but the best for the old man.

They must have made changes to The Ivanhoe* since the time I was in there. I can't remember anything scary about the dungeon- but maybe I don't scare easily.

I had a letter from the lawyer the other day and he tells me the divorce will be absolute sometime this month. That will be the best news I've had this year. He claims he had quite a time with her before she was willing to go through with it. I suppose she decided to let the whole business drop, because she wasn't interested in anyone else at the time.*

I took an insurance policy out the other day for ten thousand. It will cost me almost seven dollars a month, but I figure it is money well spent while there is a war going on. You can never tell about those bullets.

I haven't had a letter from Brownie for quite a while now. I suppose he will be writing one of these days soon. I wonder why he hasn't written you. He has a lot in common with Frank when it comes to writing letters. Speaking of Frank, it's been quite a while since he last wrote. Is he going back to his old ways again or is he just waiting for the news to pile up?

The boys in the company have been doing a lot of fishing these last two weeks. Getting some good-sized amberjacks too. One of the fellows shot a sea bass that must have been about sixty pounds or so. Plenty big he was.* I haven't been out to try my luck as yet. It's always plenty of time and no ambition or plenty of ambition and no time. I'll have to get organized on that soon.

It's been two weeks since I last played golf and it's a good bet it will be a lot more than two weeks before I play again.

Have been on all night telephone duty recently and it has been swell. We have a good radio in the day room and I've been catching up on my musical education. Have listened to WGN and WBBM several times and what a treat to hear the bands from Chicago give with the music.

There is nothing new on that transfer to the Air Corps that I have been working on. I can't do a thing until my birth certificate gets here and it seems to be slow in coming. I guess the folks aren't exactly crazy about the idea.*

35

That just about covers everything so I will close for now. Weather is still perfect, health is still perfect, and the Spanish is getting harder and harder.

Say "Hello" to all for me and write soon.

As Ever,
Joe

Did you give Eleanore my address? I've been sort of waiting to hear from her.

J

---

*The Ivanhoe, located at 3000 N. Clark in Chicago, was a speakeasy during Prohibition, and later a dinner theater. The building resembles a castle, hence Joe's reference to the dungeon. Today the building houses a Binny's Liquor store.

*It appears my dad "dodged a bullet" by getting divorced and I will always wonder how {he} a nice guy like him ever got mixed up with her.
Mary Jo

*Fish were abundant, however, while they swam or spear fished, one man would stand guard against sharks hiding in the reef.

*My dad always loved planes and passed that love on to me. I was very sad to learn that he was serious about going into the Air Corps and my grandmother squelched that dream by never sending him his birth certificate.
Mary Jo

Thursday, the 23rd
Dear John and Lou,

Forgive me for neglecting to answer you for so long, but things have been moving along pretty fast these last few days and I just haven't had the opportunity.

I hope that you can manage to get along without that scorecard you sent me. I won't be able to return it to you as it looks too much like a number code and the censor won't pass it. It seems to me that you won't have any need for it though. At least I hope so.

I'll bet it will almost be like old times going to the Lions Club to bowl.* I sure wish I could be there.

I still haven't heard from Brownie. It's been more than a month since I last heard from him and it looks like it will be a lot more than another month before he gets around to writing. I sure hope he is more prompt in writing to Baldy, or I'll probably never hear from the Eagle again.* You might ask Frank why he finds it necessary to wait for a letter from Brown before writing. He really does write a swell letter on his own. He must have a complex about writing letters.

I still can't give you any news about the Air Corps. I have written home time and again for my birth certificate and I can't get a word on the subject from the folks. About the only thing I can figure out is that my mother still has those silly notions about flying. If you should by any chance happen to see any of the family you might give them a little pep talk and see if that gets any results. It's really too bad they won't cooperate as I think I would stand a fair chance of making the grade.

I bet you are all tickled that the warm weather has finally come to stay. It must be a welcome relief after the cold. Personally, I wouldn't mind a little snow and ice, not too much of it though, I don't think I could take it after all this warmth. All of which is just another way of saying the weather is still as nice as ever out here.

I finally got some pictures made. I've got a set of prints for you on order that I should get in a few days and I'll send them then. I'm not sure they will get through the censors, but I'll try. They were developed at the post photography shop and have already passed the post censor so I don't think I'll have too much trouble with them.

I'm expecting to go to the race track next Sunday and I'll take some pictures there and send them later.

I wonder if this letter will get to you before you move? Don't forget to send me the Dickens address in your next letter. Come to think of it, after you move, I'll be writing to all four of you guys at once. I won't have much to say about Frank's not writing then, will I?

Did you ever give Eleanore my address? I have been sort of expecting to hear from her, but no luck yet.

Where are Tony and Laura going to move? Say hello to them for me and tell John to give Laura a kiss for me. He should like that.

There's an awful lot of things that have happened this last week, but censorship makes it pretty hard to write about. I guess I'll just have to save it until after the war and tell you about it then.

I can't think of anything else, so I will close for now. Say "Hello" to all for me and write soon.

As Ever,
Joe

*Joe remained a member of the Lions Club for many years after the war. I remember well the yearly Lion's fund raiser and the numerous rolls of hard candy at Helen and Joe's house. Joe also continued to bowl on leagues for many years.
Geri

*Lions Candy Day was always in October, and as a result my dad would buy the leftover candy to pass out at Halloween. It was a never ending source of embarrassment for me as kid.
Mary Jo

*The Eagle- yet another nickname for Frank (aka Baldy)

Wednesday

Dear John and Lou,

Your swell letter got here today and I sure was glad to hear from you. Seems like your letters don't come often enough these days.

I'm listening to Dick Jurgens and his gang from the Aragon * as I sit here and write this. I'm on all night duty as telephone operator and there is a swell radio here in the orderly room. This is the first night work I've ever had to do that I really enjoy. Heard Bob Hope and Red Skelton earlier in the evening and now it is solid dance music. It's hard to describe the feeling I get when I listen to Dick or Laurence Welk. Seems almost like being back home in the living room.

It's now twelve fifteen and some guy by the name of Forester has just come on from The Stevens* I've never heard of him.

I had a letter from Brownie the other day and from the tone of it he is all for the army life. Claims the only thing he misses is Al.* He is in the signal section and should he stay there he is in a pretty good spot I would say.

I was glad to hear that you were looking forward to a nice Easter. I hope everything worked out as you expected it to.

Our Easter out here was just another day. Work went on as usual and except for the fact that a chaplain came out from the post to hold services there was nothing about the day to distinguish from any other. We sure do have bad luck with the holidays. Christmas on the train, New Years on the boat and now Easter.

I'm sort of anxious to hear if you can make your lead stand up in the pinochle club, Lou. Knowing how you like to bowl, I would hate to see the heel catch you on the homestretch. Last time I bowled was in Abilene, Texas before we left the States. All of which reminds me that it has been three months since we got here in Panama. It don't seem that long.

I guess you will have to wait a few weeks before starting that album. We took some pictures last week and sent them in to be developed, but I don't know how long it will be before we get back to the post and I'll be able to send them. I'll send them as soon as possible.

Am listening to an all-night station from New York and they sure are playing some swell records. Reminds me of the nite watch from W.I.N.D

Did Eleanore have a nice visit in Chicago? Sure wish I could have been there.

Can't seem to concentrate on writing tonight with all that swell music in my ears. It's taken me two hours to write this much.

I hear you're having a bunch of swell weather back home. It's still nice as ever out here.

About the Spanish- it's gotten along swell up to a certain point and all of a sudden it gets hard. It will probably take a little longer, but I'll get there.

I had an idea my golf scores would be received with a grain of salt by the boys. Sure wish I had them here as I've got an idea that in my present shape I could teach them a few tricks. I suppose by the time you get this letter you'll just about be ready to move. That sounds like it should work out swell. I mean you moving in together with Frank and Kay.

If nothing turns up to prevent it, I expect to go fishing tomorrow afternoon. We are near the ocean and I hear tell that some of the boys have been coming back with some good-sized amberjack and tarpon. A couple of us are going out to try our luck. I suppose I'll have to send pictures of anything we might catch in order to convince certain people.

Damn, I'm going to give up on this letter for tonight. I've been sitting here for three hours and can't get started. I hate to turn off the radio with all that swell music coming out. Just heard Bing sing "Deep in the Heart of Texas." What a record!

Will close for now with a promise to do better next time. I hope to have some real news next time I write. Say "Hello" to all for me and write soon.

As Ever,
Joe

The suntan and the health are still as good as ever.
J

*Opened in 1926, The Aragon was a popular dance hall in Chicago. The interior was designed to look like a Mediterranean Plaza, with a ceiling painted to look like the sky with stars moving across it. In 1927, WGN Radio began live broadcasting, making the Aragon Ballroom famous nationwide. Later, in the 1960's, after a decline in social dancing, the Aragon began to host rock concerts.

*Opened in 1927, The Stevens Hotel on South Michigan Avenue is the former name of the famous Chicago Hilton.

*Al is Brownie's wife Alberta

Sunday, May 10, 1942

Dear John and Lou,

Received your letter yesterday and it was good hearing from you again, even tho your letter was so brief. Don't be worried about writing me long letters as long as you're in such a stew about moving. I understand the mess you're in and I don't expect many letters until you get straightened out.

Your living together with Frank and Kay is going to make writing a letter much simpler for all of us. You, because there will be four of you to do the writing and I, because I will be able to write two letters in one. It's not that I haven't the time or the inclination, but most everything we do is confidential and can't be written about. Sometimes it gets pretty hard finding enough news to write a letter.

So, you heard that Eleanore had written me? She sent a nice letter and closed with the hope I wouldn't be as long in answering as I was in writing, so I answered the same day.

Were you the first ones to move from Winona? I mean, do Joy and Janet and Tony and Laura still live there, or did they move before you did? I'll bet you were just a little bit sorry to leave there. Couldn't help feeling a little bad about leaving a place as nice as yours was. But living with the "Fireside Kids" should be even better. It just occurred to me- living together that way will make it a lot easier on the boys. They will be able to get along on one car and with tires so hard to get that will go an awful lot in the long run.*

Went to Panama City again last Sunday to try my luck with the hay burners and came out second best.

43

They didn't hurt me much, but they didn't do me any good either.

Have the boys been over to the house lately? I've had a feeling these past two weeks that there is something wrong. I know they are kept plenty busy, but for some reason I have the feeling there is something wrong that they won't write me about. If John should happen to be in the neighborhood- I would appreciate it if he stopped in and said hello. Don't say anything about my writing you. Just see how everyone is and write me.

I'm still waiting to hear from friend Brownie. He must be awfully busy learning about radio not to have the time to drop a guy a line.

I had hoped to be able to send you those oft promised pictures in this letter, but it looks like they will have to wait until next time. They should be here by Wednesday and I'll send them right along. At any note- the wait was well worth the while, because there are some beautiful shots in the group. If you decide to keep an album, let me know and I'll keep sending more from time to time.

One of the boys wrote a poem the other day and I think you would get a laugh out of it, so I'm sending it along.

Last nite was the big night for the pinochle club- wasn't it? Did you have a good time bowling at the Lions Club? I sat around last night and thought of you guys bowling and how I would have liked to be there with you.

Well, I'm starting to run out of time and space, so I will close for now. Say "Hello" to all for me and write as soon as you get back to normal.

As Ever,
Joe

How is the weather back home? Should be like midsummer by now. We are still enjoying perfect weather. Looks like it will never change.
What the hell is the matter with the Sox? It's taking them even longer to get started this year than last. Once they start winning those games that they have been losing by one run they should be alright.

Joe

*The main reason the U.S. was having a rubber shortage was because the Japanese had conquered Malaya and the Dutch East Indies, who produced most of the world's rubber, thus eliminating 91% of America's rubber supply. From January 1942 through December 1945, tires and rubber goods were rationed. Each civilian automobile was allowed five tires for the duration of the war. Certificates for new tires were restricted to vehicles for public health and safety, essential trucking, and public transportation. Civilians needed permission from their local tire board to get tires recapped. Gas rationing was actually intended to reduce driving in order to save tires. Macy's traditional Thanksgiving Day Parade was cancelled from 1942-1944. In 1942, Macy's donated their parade balloons to the war effort in a public ceremony.

I could tell you that I wrote this myself, but you wouldn't believe it and I'm not here to bluff, so I didn't. But the typewriting is my own handicraft. Inspired by the Tales of the Bushmaster which roams this neck of the woods is a little poem I hope you will find interesting. This pathetic tale is to be read in all seriousness and with sympathetic understanding for the unfortunate hero of our drama .

The Tale
Into the jungle one summer day
A lonely soldier chanced to stray
Far from home and sweetheart kind
He sought surcease from a troubled mind
So into the jungle wild and wet
He hacked his way with a heavy machete
He came at last to a winding path
That led through the jungle's might swath
As he strode along in sad dismay
His troubled mind was far away
Till he raised his eyes and they came in line
With a tangled mass of jungle vine
There not three feet from his startled face
A huge bushmaster was saying grace
To the rear he marched and his arms did flail
As he left behind a smoking trail
The curves were short but he made them long
And the trees went down with a mournful song
He passed from the jungle into the light of day
But a strip of ocean barred his way
He hit the water like a flying fish
And the strip went dry like a broken dish
As he climbed the shore in a terrific grind

He filled the hole he left behind
The sentry who sought to hold the gate
With military honors now lies in state
The guard was formed to stand retreat
As he steered a course for his company street
The ranks exploded with a crushing sound
Like a ton of bricks dumped on the ground
Down the field the guardsman fluttered
Like the falling leaves in the time of autumn
And the breeze he made as he ambled past
Stripped the OD of all his brass
Beneath his bunk he dived from sight
Paper rustled and he died from fright

Friday, May 15, 1942

Dear John and Lou,

Found your swell letter waiting for me when I got in yesterday and it sure was good hearing from you. It was rather unexpected tho-I didn't think you would be writing for a few days at least. Your letter got here at a good time tho. I was going to write you today and at long last send some of those oft promised pictures. Now I'll kill two birds with one stone. The pictures I had hoped to send didn't get in yesterday (the ones with me on them), but I did get a lot of good scenic shots to start that album with. I'm sort of depending on you to do that, Lou. I know you will like the idea and they will make a lot of conversation when this is all over. I've got quite a few pictures here-too many to send at one time, so I'll send some along with each letter.

I had a letter from Eleanore yesterday and she's getting along as well as ever. She tells me she's been given another raise. First thing you know- she will have to start worrying about fortune hunters. She was sort of wondering why she hasn't been hearing from you lately. She guessed (and rightly too) that you are in a mess at home and don't have much time for letters.

Too bad about all the trouble you are having getting into your new home. It must be pretty tough-having to move in two jumps. I can sympathize with you, having gone through quite a few moving days myself. But are you certain the reason you haven't been to a show is too much work? I haven't seen a picture in over three weeks now. And it will probably be another week or so before our theater is finished. I sure would enjoy seeing a good picture again.

48

I'm still waiting to hear from Brownie. Of all the double plated drips- that guy takes the cake.

I wonder if he's as long in writing Al as he is in writing us. By the way - how is she? So, you see her anymore? Or has she gone back to her folks?

Say, Lou- ask the boys how that Friday night business of theirs is getting along? I don't expect an answer to that question, but I thought I would ask. I understand that the only men left are the over age and the helpless ones (at least that's how Eleanore finds it in New York). So, they must be doing a good Friday night business these days.

There is still a shortage of things to write about. I didn't go into Panama City last week and while I probably saved money it deprived me of the one thing I could write about. You're probably tired of hearing of the races tho, so it's just as well. Unless something turns up to prevent my going, I hope to get in next Sunday and try my luck again. I just had an idea. I think I'll send you a copy of the Panama paper. It's a little different from the papers we have at home and you might get a kick out of it. I hear you're having a lot of damp and chilly weather back home. It's taking longer than usual to settle down this year-isn't it?

I was thinking of you and John last night. I sure would have liked being with you on your anniversary, but as you said, we'll have all the more to celebrate when I get back.

I've got just about enough time to go down to the creek and do a little swimming before dark, so I will close for now.

Say "Hello" to everyone for me and write as soon as you can.

As Ever,
Joe

Am sending a dozen pics. Be sure to let me know how many you get.
J

Wednesday, May 20, 1942

Hello John, Lou, Frank, Kay, and Milly,

Came in a few moments ago and found your swell letter waiting for me. It was good hearing from you and in such a short time. It's been only three days since I had your last letter. I guess you're one letter behind because, you ask for the pictures and they have been on the way for the past week. I guess you have them by now. I hope you weren't too disappointed (not that it's a disappointment) at not finding any pictures of me in the bunch. I guess I must be under an unlucky star or something, because I'm having a lot of trouble getting some pictures of myself. I had hoped to get them in time to mail in this letter, but our post exchange will be closed for the next two days as its being moved to a new location and I was unable to get them. I'm sending another dozen assorted shots tho, and I hope they will keep you content until next letter. By the way - How did you like the pics I sent? I think they are plenty good and I'm hoping you enjoyed looking at them. I've got quite a few pictures in my locker and I'm having a hell of a time trying to remember which prints I sent you. Don't be too surprised if you get two of the same pictures. I suppose I should have some kind of a system, but it's too hot to think too much.

We've been plenty busy these last two days. Yesterday was moving day again and today is straightening up day. No- it's not what you're probably thinking. We are still in the same camp. All we did was move out of the tents and into the barracks. Things are coming along nicely, and in another week or so it will be almost like home. We're still doing our bathing in the river, but the water should be turned on in the shower rooms most any day now and that will be the biggest thing that could happen to us. Our theater building has been completed for the last two days now but they are having a little trouble getting some parts for the sound equipment, so it will be a few more days before we will have a picture to go to at night. There's supposed to be a band concert over there tonight, so I guess I'll walk over and see what goes.

I know you will find this rather hard to believe, but I - me in person, went to church Sunday. That made the third Sunday in a row. Lt. Sampson (the chaplain) is a good friend of mine and a swell fellow and I don't know for certain yet whether I'm going to church to please him or because I want to go. Regardless- I can't say that going has done me any harm.

Of course, I went right in to Panama City Sunday afternoon and tried my best to erase any benefits I might get from going to church. Went to the races again and while the luck wasn't so good it wasn't so bad either. I just about broke even. I saw something that very seldom occurs at a track. A horse (Ace Fessenden by name) went out and won a race very easily and after crossing the finish line, just fell over and died. I think it was the first race he ever won and he couldn't stand the shock.

Wonder of wonders- I finally met an honest to goodness white gal. Asked her for a date and she agreed. I almost passed out. I'm not going to say too much about it yet as I have a healthy suspicion the young lady won't show up. But if everything goes off well I'll write you the bloody details.

I see I'm just about out of space, so I will start to close for now. Say "Hello" to everyone for me and write soon.

As Ever,
Joe

Can't think of a suitable way of addressing a letter to five of you so I'll just keep on in the old way but you can consider it as being written to all of you. And Lou, I wouldn't be saying too much about the Sox. Seven in a row and the end still not in sight isn't bad. Weather and health are still perfect. Hope this letter finds all of you the same.
J

Thursday, May 27, 1942

Dear John, Lou, Frank, Kay and Milly,

That's rather a long greeting-don't you think? I guess I'll shorten it to "Hello Gang" next time.

Don't hold it against me for being so long in answering. The last three days have been busier than usual and I just haven't had a chance to even start a letter. I've got a half a dozen here all of them waiting to be answered and I don't know when I'll be able to get to them.

We have been out on a problem the last two days and it's been one of the most interesting experiences I ever hope to have. Too bad I can't tell you about it, but it's been the first of its kind I've ever been on. It will be another good story to tell you when I get back.*

Of all things-They made a radio man out of me for the problem. I went to school for a few hours the other day and had a few lessons in operation and finally wound up today carrying a Walkie Talkie. They're pretty simple to operate and certainly do a good job at communication.

So glad to hear that you enjoyed the pictures. Did you get the second group I sent? Most of them have a story or an experience behind them and they will make some nice remembrances.

Leave it to me to ball up the job tho. I had so many pics in my locker when I first started sending them and I didn't keep track of which pictures I sent you. (I had two prints of each, one for you and one for the folks) so that now I'm not sure of which ones I sent you and which ones I didn't. If you should happen to get two prints of the same picture, just have John stop at the house and exchange it for another one.

Looks like the army is catching up with everyone. How come Mac is joining? Is he as patriotic as all that? At that rate there won't be many males left.

I'm still without a word from Brownie. I've given up on the guy completely. I don't care if I ever hear from him. Should be a letter from Eleanore tomorrow. It doesn't take a letter quite as long to make a round trip from here to New York. Not quite so far and better service.

Well, gang- it's been an awfully long day and I'm just a little tired, so I'll cut this letter short. I promise to do a better job next time. Say "Hello" to all for me and write soon.

As ever,
Joe

Too bad about the miserable weather you're having. I wish I could send you some of ours.
J

Almost forgot to thank you for the swell pencils you sent. I wrote this letter with one of them. I gave the others to my company commander. He got a big kick out of it. I've had about fifty people ask me for one of them.
J

*From my research, I have reason to believe this may have been a mission of espionage. Unfortunately, this story went to the grave with my father.
Mary Jo

Wednesday June 3, 1942

Hello John, Lou, Frank, Kay and Milly,

That's the longest heading I ever expected to start a letter with. I think I will use two lines next time and include everyone. Found your letter waiting for me when I came in this noon and I don't have to tell you how glad I was to hear from you.

Glad the pictures all arrived in good shape and that all of you got such a kick out of them. The only thing you forgot to tell me was how many you received. Not counting these I am sending in this letter I have sent you exactly thirty-six. Be sure to tell me how many you received as I am anxious to know how many of them the censors held back-if any.

I am enclosing the rest of the pics I have around, but they are not quite as good as the ones I have already sent. I'm expecting to get another bunch from the studio by the end of the week and there are some beauties in that bunch. (including some of myself which nobody would call beauties except myself) and I'll send them on in the next letter.

They just finished paying the boys off and right now there are more poker and dice games going on than you can shake a stick at. Some guy no doubt will wind up with a big bundle of lettuce, while a dozen others will be broke before morning. Funny how a bunch of soldiers can go around just about broke for two weeks of the month and then lose their pay inside of a day.

What goes with your moving? You're certainly getting a run around. I suppose by now you're all adjusted on Kimball and moving will be just that much harder.

I had a letter from Eleanore the other day and that gal is sure doing alright for herself. I suppose she has

56

written you that she is going to move in with one of the girls from her office whose husband has been called into service. She told me about an affair she went to. A company luncheon or something and of all things she was called on to make a speech. I couldn't help but be reminded how John and I used to get her so flustered she couldn't even talk.

We are still waiting for the theater to be opened. They have been working on it for the last three days and with a little luck we should see a show this weekend.

I still haven't heard a word from Brownie. Try and figure out some people.

Went to town again last Sunday. The same old story-went to the track and then into town for a few hours. The date fell through. No fault of the gals. I just couldn't get into town that day. I went over and explained and I hope to try again a week from Sunday. Will write you the details if and when it ever comes off. I'm doing my best to write this letter but they are putting some strong temptation under my nose. I don't think I can hold out much longer so I may as well close for now.

There's a rumor around that you're having some swell weather in Chicago these days. Any truth in it? There is a new censor regulation which forbids us from even mentioning the weather, so you will just have to guess from now on.

Well, gang- I really will close this time. Say "Hello" to everyone for me and don't forget to write soon.

As ever,
Joe

Wednesday, June 10, 1942

Dear John, Lou, Frank, Kay and Milly-

Here's that long headline again. I started to tear up this page, but happened to think of the paper shortage so decided to let it go just this once. Next time I'll find a shorter or better way of starting the letter.

I got your letter yesterday and it sure was good hearing from you again. I guess the service must be getting better. It didn't seem to take the letters so long to make the round trip this time.

Frank's getting his occupational questionnaire certainly was a bit of news. I'm afraid I'm not up to snuff on the occupational part of it tho. I gather that all they wanted to know was what kind of work does he do. Whether he is vital to defense. Give me more news about it the next time you write. What does Baldy think about it all. Does he expect to be called? I guess he's not expecting to be called soon or you wouldn't be making plans to leave on your vacation the end of this month. Isn't it strange the way they've gotten to Frank before they got to John? I can't figure out the workings of a draft board.

Had a letter from home yesterday and it seems like you're not the only ones I sent duplicate pictures to. I wasn't a bit surprised. In fact- I was almost positive that I had sent two of the same. The way I had them mixed up I'm surprised that there weren't more.

I've still got a few left and I'm sending them in this letter. One of the fellows took some pictures of me last week (the ones I promised to send in this letter) and they came back Monday with nothing on them. He must have exposed the film to the sunlight or something. I sent some more in yesterday and I should have some of them the next time I write.

You must have been looking forward to big things, Suzy. I mean when you went out and bought all those new corners. I don't know if I'll be able to send that many snaps, but I'll try.

Well, at long last our theater is going to open up. We'll be seeing our first picture next Friday night and to say that every one of us is looking forward to it would be an understatement of fact. Don't know much about what kind of pictures we will be seeing, but one of them will be James Cagney in- "Captains of the Clouds." How long has it been showing in Chicago? I don't think it's too old.

You ask me how many people I'm writing to. Well- there's you of course, and home. Then there are two fellows who were at Camp Wolters with me. One here in the Zone and one in Chicago. He lives on the South Side and was discharged because of a bad eye.* Then there is Eleanore. And two girls in Fort Worth that I hope to see again when this is all over. I almost forgot Verla. That makes eight plus one from Annabelle once in a while and even Evelyn. It's a hell of a lot of letters to be writing for a guy who wouldn't know news if it were in the same bed with him. There is still a shortage of news out here. It's been early to bed and early to rise all this week. All routine stuff-nothing exciting. The weather has been perfect this last week. All in all, I haven't a complaint.

I see I'm about to run out of space so I will close for now. Give my best to all and write soon.

As ever,
Joe

I'm expecting a letter from El most any day now. I suppose she is having her troubles too, what with moving and all. If you see Tony and Laura, say "Hello" for me. Will you?

*My mother grew up in Hyde Park on the South Side of Chicago. The word always was that my parents met through the mail by writing letters during the war. Could this friend from the South Side have been the link that connected my parents?
Mary Jo

Tuesday, June 23, 1942

Hi Gang,

You certainly were a long time in writing your last letter. I kept hoping it would get here but wasn't too disappointed when it was so late as I know you were head over heels in work with moving and whatnot. It sure was good hearing from you again.

I'm trying to make up my mind about this letter. I don't know if it will get to Chicago in time to catch you before you leave on your vacation. I've got a few more pictures I was intending to send, but I can't make up my mind whether to send them now or wait till you get back.

So, you finally heard from Brownie. I still haven't had a letter from him and don't intend to write him until I get one. I'll be looking forward to getting Frank's letter with all the details.

Sorry about that picture with no creases in the pants, but what can you expect from a pair of coveralls? Wait until you get a load of me in khaki. You _will_ be surprised.

I'll bet you're glad to be practically settled down again. You sure make it sound good. I hope you stay there long enough to give me a chance to see the place.

I certainly was surprised to hear that Mike is in uniform. What the hell do they want old Peachfuzz in the army for? They must be getting hard up for men or something.

I still can't make up my mind whether to make this a short letter and no picture or vice versa. I guess I may as well enclose the snaps. They might just as well lay in your mailbox as my footlocker.

It's been so long since I last wrote you I can't remember what I wrote about. Did I tell you that our theater has finally opened and that it makes camp life about one hundred percent better.

The pictures haven't all been of the best, but there have been several good ones in the bunch. We saw "Captains of the Clouds" last week. I thought it was swell. Also had Marlene Dietrich in "The Lady Is Willing." Liked that a lot too. Then Sunday we saw Leslie Howard in "Mr. V." On the schedule for tomorrow is "Woman of the Year" and for Sunday, "Ball of Fire." I'm looking forward to both of them. That's about enough of theater schedules and pictures. As good as a theater is for our pleasure, well that's about as good as our steel spring cots and mattresses are for our comfort. That's a little news I don't think I've written you about. The army came across with them last week and what a welcome relief from the canvass cots we have been sleeping on these many months. They are almost <u>too</u> comfortable. I have a hard time getting up when I lay down.

I went to Panama again last Sunday as per custom and had the usual time. It's getting to be a routine-this business of going to the races and then spending the evening in town. I did have a little bit more luck than usual tho. Another fellow and I won thirty dollars between us. In the round of the joints we visited in the evening I picked up a few of those drink mixers. As soon as I can figure out a way of sending them without breaking them to bits I'll do so. They will make nice souvenirs (at least Lou will think so).

By the way- Did you ever get the paper I sent you? You have never mentioned it.

Where are you going on your vacation? Out to Phillip's and Pletzke's?* I wish I could spend a week or two with you. Can't think of anything I would rather do. Have a good time and don't write me any fish stories unless you send pictures along to prove it.

Had a letter from Eleanore the other day. I'm afraid I'll have to agree with you that she's doing all right.

I suppose she has written you about her change in vacation plans in order to be in Chicago for Bernadine's wedding so I won't say any more about it. I did sort of rib her a little on the breaking up of the old maids' club. I hope she didn't take it too seriously. You know how different words are on paper. Especially when I write them.

Well, Gang- I think I've done too much scribbling already, so I will close for now. Be sure to send me your vacation address. Say "Hello" to everyone for me and write soon.

As ever,
Joe

I would like to hear from Tony and Laura again. Tell them to write me when you see them again.

*We assume this a reference to a family resort on Long Lake in Phillips, Wisconsin.

Wednesday, July 23, 1942
Hello Gang,

I was just beginning to despair of ever hearing from you again when your post cards and letter finally arrived. I was going to write you at Eagle River, but since your cards arrived here only three days ago there wasn't enough time, so I decided to wait until you got back home. Sure was glad to hear that you had such a good time on your trip. I wonder how long it will be before I can make a trip like that again. Begins to look as tho it will be a couple of years at best. Oh well, I guess the place will still be there.

I had an idea that my last letter would get to your house just a few days after you left. I'm glad you liked the pictures. Make the most of them as it's just possible that they may be the last you get for a long time. A lot of things have happened since I last wrote. Many things in fact, that I'm not certain of what I wrote you in my last letter. The most important bit of news is our new change of address. I thought I wrote you about it, but since your last letter was addressed to the old address I guess maybe I didn't. I got it down at the end of the letter. Be sure you don't lose it as I don't know how long it will take a letter with the old address to get to me. The new address explains a lot of things. The main reason for it being is to keep our whereabouts a little more secret. It also means that I won't be able to send you the souvenirs I wrote you about, because they have names of places on them. The same applies to pictures. Course, I'll still be able to send you some pictures, but they won't be the same as those I've already sent. We haven't heard any more about it since being given the new address, so I don't think we will be moving to a new location. However, you can't tell about those things. We may be gone by the time this letter reaches you.

Had a letter from El last week and the poor gal is sure in a dither about this moving business. Seems like every letter I get from her has a new address on it.

I had no idea that Al and Ruby went along with you on your vacation. Why didn't Baldy ask Janet along and make the party complete? You really should have had her along because Frank and she get along so well together. By the way, speaking of Joy and Janet. Do you ever hear from them? I suppose you see very little of them since they moved south.

I'm afraid I don't understand all the plans you are making. I mean going to the lake for a few days and possibly going back to Eagle River. Hasn't the gas and tire rationing been put into effect around Chicago yet? I thought that the gas rationing went into effect throughout the state, but I guess I must be wrong.

Did you find any news from the draft board in your mailbox when you got back? I wonder how long it will be before you two guys get caught in the draft.

Even after three weeks of not writing you there is a usual shortage of news. Plenty of things happening all the time, but very few of them that will pass the censor.

After all that time with no show to go to, it sure was a treat when they finally opened the place. Now we have our choice of two shows every day. Good things come in bunches I guess. For instance, last night I went to the show and saw a swell picture, "A Great Man's Lady" and then stopped at the gym to see a basketball game and finally wound up in the bowling area. It made a very enjoyable evening and town seems rather a waste of time when you can do all those things right on the post. As soon as we can figure out a way to get some golf clubs we'll be out on the course trying our luck.

Well, I've been rambling on just about long enough for one letter so I will close for now. Say "Hello" to _all_ for me and write soon.

As ever,
Joe

The new address is: PvT. Joe Brill 360 35316
Co G 158th INF
APO 827 c/o Postmaster
New Orleans, LA.

Wednesday, August 12, 1942 (Joe's Birthday)
Hello John, Lou, Frank and Kay,

You hit the nail right on the head. I was just about to start losing faith in your ever writing again when your letter finally arrived. I was making allowances for all the work you had waiting for you when you got back from your vacation, but didn't think it would take this long. I forgot to make allowances for the boys-I see they are still taking two months to do two days' work. Anyway. It was swell hearing from you again.

I wonder if you got all of my letters. Your cards came too late for me to answer you in Wisconsin so I waited a few days and wrote to Chicago. Did you get the letters containing the pictures? Let me know next letter as I'm wondering if the censor got hold of them. I've had some more pictures come in since I last wrote and I'm going to try and send them in this letter. With the new censorship regulations in effect we can't send but very few pictures, but I'm going to try. I finally got the pictures of myself back from the developers. They didn't all turn out, but there were four of them that are probably as good as I'll ever take. I didn't order but one print until I could see the results, so you will have to wait until next letter for your set. I've already sent the first ones to the folks.

Speaking of the folks, I had a letter from them yesterday and they are on their vacation and having a swell time. They were asking about you, why haven't you stopped over and said Hello. I haven't written them as yet, but that's one question I'm afraid I don't know the answer to.

I hear the weather hasn't been of the best the past week or two. Had a letter from a fellow who was in camp with me down in Texas and he was crying the blues about the weather.

Things have been even busier than usual around here this last week. Seems like it's been nothing but eat, sleep, and work. I haven't even been to the show since Saturday. Missed the races last Sunday for the first time in a long time. There is a very interesting story to tell in connection with my missing out. I can't tell you about it now, but save this letter and someday I'll tell you all about it.

I had a letter from Eleanore the other day and she told me all about her trip to Chicago to visit you. If I could only get there for a week or two it would be almost like old home week. More than almost, it would be old home week.

I'm waiting anxiously for the pictures to get here. I sure hope you are going to give me more details about the big one that got away. The folks wrote me about the big ones they are getting, but I'm not saying much about that until I see the pictures.

Well, Gang - It's getting late and I'm a little more tired than usual tonight, so I will say goodbye for now.

Give my best to everyone and don't take as long with your next letter as you did with your last.

As ever,
Joe

Tuesday, September 1, 1942
Hello Gang,

I suppose I should start this letter with a hell of a bawling out for your not writing for so long, but it was so good to hear from you again. I just can't get a good mad up. Maybe it was the peace offering you sent or maybe it's the fact that today was payday that has me in such good humor-I don't know.

I just left a hot poker game fifteen dollars ahead to write this letter. It's one way of staying ahead and then too, it's been so long since I last wrote you that you're probably wondering what's happening.

I had a letter from Eleanore the other day and she says she had a swell time, and no doubt she did, but with all the running around she did it seemed to me it was more like staying in New York and working rather than going on a vacation. She also told me that you showed her the letter I wrote her and that you made a lot of funny noises about my telling her you hadn't written in some time. What could I say to that-nothing but the truth so I wrote her back and told her again, just the same as when I last saw her. Seemed to me that John didn't have his usual summer tan. Was the weather that bad? The two man-eating pike were beauties, but how do I know who caught them? All I can see on the pictures are two fish being held up by someone, but all I can see of that someone is his right arm. Sure you didn't take a picture of someone else? While I'm on the subject of pictures-I'm glad you liked the last bunch I sent. I've got another group here, but I won't send them until next letter as I have only one stamp and won't be able to get anymore until tomorrow. I've got four of yours truly and I'm going to drop them in this letter for your approval.

The last letter I had from home the folks told me that John had stopped at the house to see about the summer home. I got to thinkin' of the fun we used to have out there and first thing you know I was getting that homesick feeling. They also mentioned that Mr. Daum and Frank Nehr had stopped in to say Hello to them while they were on their vacation.

You made John and Frank's coming into the service sound pretty definite. If I had to do it all over again I would pick the branch of service I think I would like the best and enlist for the duration before I let them draft me. It's pretty hard to get transferred to another branch after you're in (At least it is out here) and doing something you like makes army life a lot easier. I've met quite a few sailors and they make the navy sound like not a bad place to be in.

I'm still without a word from Brownie. Lord only knows where he's been sent to by this time, but that's hardly an excuse for not writing. If that's his attitude, the hell with him.

This has been a plenty busy day so far. We went on our weekly conditioning hike this morning and got paid this afternoon. Things are pretty quiet now except for the usual card and dice games. More money being won and lost every hour than you can shake a stick at.

I'm looking forward to going to town this coming Sunday and taking in the races. I missed out last week and it's bothering me already. Going to town isn't so important as long as there is the show go to every nite. We've been seeing a good grade of entertainment these past two weeks, pictures like

"Syncopation," The "Sabateur", "My Favorite Blonde" and "Rings on her Finger." With picks like that to be seen every nite there's no sense in leaving camp.

When and if I ever get out of this army I don't think I'll care to see a show for a couple of months at least.

Well Gang - It's just about time for chow call, so I'll say goodbye for now. If I can get some stamps I'll send the rest of the pictures in a day or two. So, until later -

As ever,

Joe

Don't be as long answering this letter as you were the last or I'll come and get you.

J

Saturday, September 11, 1942

Hi Gang,

Seems like every time I start a letter to you lately I'm either raising hell because you're not so prompt on the answers or I'm apologizing for not writing sooner myself. I guess there won't be any more delays on your end, so if I can get myself straightened out everybody should be happy. The way we have been working these last few weeks it's all to do to find time to write a letter.

I'm glad you liked the pictures I sent. Personally, I can't see anything to rave about, but if you like them I guess I haven't got any complaints. You're getting quite a collection of snaps, what? I didn't think I had sent that many. Take good care of that album cause I'm sending all the pictures I can get and I probably won't have a one beyond those I send you and the folks. I'm enclosing another dozen for your approval. Hope you like them. I've got quite a few in being developed, some of myself and more scenery and as soon as they come back I'll send them.

You've got me all wrong Suzy. I didn't seriously doubt that the fish were caught by the boys. After all, two fish to show for a three weeks' vacation is just about the boys' speed. I'll bet you got some nice bass at the summer home the four days you were out there- or did you? Soon as the pictures are developed I'll send you some shots of real fish. Sharks, catfish and stuff like that here. Some of them are so big we have to shoot them before we can land 'em.

It was sure good to hear that Grandma is getting along so well. Give her my love and tell her I can't wait until we can have another one of our rip-snorting card games. Won't be too long now.

Damn, your advice about not losing all my winnings at the races was good, but a shade too late. It got to burning holes in my pockets, so I went into town last Sunday and took quite a beating. Guess I'll stay in camp this week and recuperate.

I suppose as I write this the boys are well on their way to Minnesota. Reminds me of the trips we used to take together and makes me a little blue. But I guess Wisconsin and Minnesota will still be there when I get back.

Haven't heard from Eleanore in quite a spell, but no doubt she is busy entertaining your folks and hasn't much time for writing letters.

Well Gang- there is the usual shortage of news on this end of the line. Went on a hike yesterday morning and spent the afternoon cleaning equipment for this morning's inspection.

By the way, what did you do over Labor Day? Out fishing somewhere or I don't know the boys. We didn't even get the day off. Worked just as hard as usual if not harder. We are getting a holiday on the 16th of this month though. That's the second anniversary of the induction of the National Guard and there will be a celebration of sorts. I understand there will be a leg show at the theater (I wonder where the legs are coming from) and other forms of entertainment. Will write you more about it after it happens.

I suppose you are all getting ready for old man winter to come knocking on the door. I can't say that I envy you although I would like to get out of this heat for a while. One of those cold windy Chicago days would probably be the death of me.

Well, the boys are calling so I guess it's just about time for the second show to start.

We are seeing "*The Jungle Book*" tonight. I don't think I'm going to like it, but what the hell.

I'll say goodbye for now. Give my best to everyone and write soon.

As Ever,
Joe

Saturday September 19, 1942

Hi Gang,

I'll write this to all of you as usual, but I'm going to show a lot favoritism to Suzy.

I guess you must have written your last letter on impulse Lou, because you made no mention of getting my last letter and the pictures, so I'm looking forward to another letter in a day or two. First let me say how nice I thought your letter was and what a kick I got out of it, particularly the letter your mother added. Tell her for me that I enjoyed every word of it and say thank you. I was going to write her and do it myself, but on second thought decided against it. Since you tell her most everything I write you and since there is so very little we are allowed to write about, I would just be repeating myself.

Your remark that the family is moving around a lot these days was an understatement of fact if I ever heard one. Cold weather and gas rationing will be slowing you up and I'll bet you will be glad of the chance to settle down for a few months. Don't forget to send me the pictures of the fishing trip - particularly the fish, if any.

I was called to headquarters this morning and given the nicest job you will ever see. I had long ago given up all hopes of ever doing any work in the army concerning decorating, but I have been proven wrong. We have one hundred and thirty-five new hardwood tables for the mess hall and it's up to me to see that they get refinished. We're going to fill and sand them and then spray two coats of pure lacquer. We've got a swell spray compressor and if the job doesn't turn out good it won't be the fault of the equipment. Seems just like old times, but at a hell of a

75

cut in wages. I wonder if it would do me any good to show a union card. I hardly think so.

Well, tomorrow's Sunday and as I'm still solvent for this month I guess it's off to the races again. I've had a bad streak this last month and I'm way overdue for some good luck.

That really was a bit of news- I mean about Joy and Janet expecting again. I'm glad to hear they are getting along so well again. Has Joy changed very much? I imagine he has now that certain influences and temptations are a little further removed. Not that he has ever needed much coaxing, but it probably did some good.

Just finished writing to Eleanore. I've been trying to find time to write her all week, but this afternoon was the first time I could manage.

Our holiday turned out to be somewhat of a flop. We had a perfect morning, but towards noon the weather soured a little and the afternoon's festivities were called off on account of.....The floor show we were to have in the evening was called off because of....I can't tell you, but we did see Abbott and Costello in "Rio Rita." I got a bang out of it.

Well children, I think I've said just about enough so I'll stop saying for now. Say "Hello" to everyone for me and write soon.

As ever,
Joe

Thursday October 8, 1942
Hi Gang,

Found your letter waiting for me when I got in this afternoon and it sure was good hearing from you so soon. I was going to answer the letter I got from New York, but there was little or nothing in the way of news, so I decided to wait until hearing from you.

When the letter from home arrived telling me that the divorce had finally been granted, I thought for a moment that at last I had some real news to write you about, but before I finished reading said letter I found that you probably know more about the whole thing than I do. What a relief to know that it's all over at last.

Give Kay my love, blessings and thanks for the help she was so willing to give. The folks were as usual very brief in telling me about the whole thing so I know practically nothing beyond the fact that they had a hard time getting her into court and that I'm a free man again.

What sort of testimony did Kay have to give? I assume that since that I was being sued for desertion that she was more or less a witness for Evelyn. Tell me all about it next letter.

So, the old girl is looking a little shopworn these days. She will probably wind up pounding the pavement one of these days. She's been heading that way for a long time and one of these days she will make the grade.

That trip to New York was rather sudden wasn't it? Must have been swell for you. You certainly did cut a wide swath for the short time you were there.

Being away from things as we are does make a difference after all. The only way I have of knowing about the rationing and things that are happening at home are the letters I get. Have they started to ration gasoline? We haven't felt rationing yet and it will be a long time before we do. When they start cutting down on us, things will be in a bad way.

What do you think of those Cardinals? We heard all the games by short wave and believe me, a lot of money changed hands when the Yankees were beaten. I noticed in the paper that the Sox won the first two games of the city series from the Cubs. It's a cinch the Cubs won't do what the Cards did. Give John my deepest sympathy. I feel for him, but can't reach him.

It's just about time for the first show to end and I don't want to miss the picture tonight. They've got Bob Hope and Madelaine Carrol in "My Favorite Blonde" and if it's half as good as they say it is, it should be plenty good. I saw Joan Bennett in "The Wife Takes a Flyer" last Sunday and if you haven't seen it yet don't miss it. Funniest thing I've seen in a long time.

I wrote Eleanore last nite. I wish now I had put it off until today. I had no idea that she wasn't feeling up to par. She hasn't said a word in her letters. I guess maybe I'll drop her another line tomorrow if I can find the time.

Well Gang- it's getting to be just about that time so I will say goodnight for now. Say "Hello" to all for me and write soon.

As ever,
Joe

Sunday, October 18

Hello Gang,

Just a line to let you know that it may be some time before you get an answer to your letter. I have been expecting it for the last few days, but it may be some time before it catches up with me. You see, I'm in the hospital. Have been since Tuesday and probably another week or so before they turn me loose. I guess the news will come as a bit of a surprise to all of you. Well. It's still a surprise to me, even after five days of being here. I woke up last Monday feeling pretty punk and when there wasn't any change Tuesday, I went to the dispensary to see what was wrong. Come to find that I had malaria* and before you could shake a stick, I was in the hospital. Spent three miserable days (I didn't much feel like writing letters or I would have written to you sooner) but am feeling as good as new again. I guess I'll be here recuperating for at least another week or so. Now that I'm feeling better I'm taking advantage of the rest to catch up on my reading and writing. It's kind of a dull life with all that time on one's hands and I'll be glad to get back to my outfit.

I've been looking forward to getting your letter (also one from the folks and Eleanore) but with having to forward them to me from my company it will probably take a little time.

Well gang- news around here is even harder to find than back in the company. About all we do is get treated, eat, lay around writing and reading, and sleep. It's a dull routine after the first few days and as I said before, I'll be glad to get back to duty.

That just about covers everything for now, gang, so I'll say so long until later. You will notice a different

79

return address on this letter, but I wouldn't write to it if I were you, because I'll probably be gone when your letter gets here and it will just be delayed in being forwarded to me. Say "Hello" to all and take your time about writing. Not too much time though.

As ever,
Joe

*Malaria is a mosquito-borne illness that attacks red blood cells and the liver. In the Pacific Theatre, malaria was prevalent and could remove a soldier from action for weeks, which is why it was considered "the other enemy."

Tuesday, October 27

Hi Gang,

Really had few hopes of getting any letters from you forwarded to me while I was in the hospital, so I can tell you it was a pleasant surprise when the ward boy came along and handed me seven of them including the two you sent. I guess you know without me telling you, how good it was to hear from you. I enjoyed every word (even what you considered the terrible letter Lou)

I guess I'll just start with the first letter and follow thru on the answers. First, let me thank you for the nice picture of the summer home. I see it hasn't changed a bit since I last saw it. At least not the front of it. The folks last letter said something about them going out to see a contractor in regards to getting the cellar dug out and made into a couple of recreation rooms. The same idea that's been talked about for so long, but I guess this time they will go thru with it. Did you know that they bought the two vacant lots next to the house? The two towards Novak's place? I've got a lot to look forward to if and when I get back home.

So, you finally heard from Brown! The card was just like the guy. You need have no fears of my saying anything to him, as I don't intend to write him until he gets around to answering my letter, and I'm not expecting him to take time out from his swimming to do that. Being in the army under circumstances such as his must be a pretty good deal. Nothing to do but swim and study with the little women hanging around to take care of all of your idle time. You know what I mean. Wish I would have a little of that kind of luck once in a while.

81

I haven't heard from Eleanore in quite some time now. Possibly there is a letter from her somewhere between the company and the hospital, but since I wrote her about a week before I wrote you I think maybe there is something wrong somewhere. I didn't bring her address along with me, so I won't be able to write her until I get back. If you should write her soon after receiving this letter ask her how come, will you?

I don't suppose you and Kay will remember the guy that I'm about to write about, but I'm pretty sure the boys remember him. Walter Lorenz. He used to do all those odd jobs for Charley Lueck when I was working for him. Well, I had a letter from him the other day. It all started when he sent a postcard to me at home telling me that he is in the army and how long would it be before they got me. The folks enclosed the card in one of their letters and I wrote him. I had the answer the other day and what a kick I got out of it. If you will recall, he had one of those droll senses of humor and it sure reflects in his letters. It was just like reading a good joke book. Was he surprised to find that I have been in the army for the last year and a half! Seems like there is an epidemic of divorces in Chicago. First me, then Gus and then Wally's letter telling me that his brother George has also gotten himself a new lease on life. His case is just like Gus, because there are two children involved. Also, I can't say that I blame George, because that wife of his was a shrew if ever I saw one.

You certainly make it sound as though it won't be very much longer before the boys' get their induction papers. With the way things are going I guess they will get everybody before very much longer. It's not all bad after the first month, so don't think about it too much. I still think the idea I wrote about not long ago is a good one. Just before you get drafted, pick yourself a branch of the service you think you would like and enlist. They have a lot of good ratings in the Air Corps and Frank wouldn't have any trouble at all making the grade as a mechanic. I would give anything to be able to do it all over again.

I suppose you're wondering a little how I'm getting along. Well, I'm as good as the day I was born, but with it all I'm still here. I'm getting a little restless of this hospital life and wish I would get returned to duty. I guess I'll go back sometime later this week.

Well Gang- I've managed to do a fair job on this letter considering that there is nothing happening around here, but I'm just about out of words so I will say goodbye for now. Give my regards and love to everyone and write soon.

As ever,
Joe

Wednesday, November 4, 1942

Hi Gang,

Going to the hospital has some merits beyond the treatment one gets. I'm talking about this sudden flood of letters that have been coming my way since I was put to bed.

I've had two letters from you since I last wrote and this is the first opportunity I've had to answer. Now that I've got a little of that precious time, I'll have to make this letter shorter than usual on account of so many to answer.

Well, it's all over at last. I was discharged from the hospital last Saturday and have been back to duty since. Sure is a grand feeling to be out in the open again. My only regret is losing all the suntan, but it won't take long to get that back. I was just a little surprised when the doctor came along and marked me for duty. Even tho I was feeling as good as ever and hoping for duty all the time, I didn't expect to be released until some day early this week. Believe me, I didn't argue the point with him.

You might tell that certain young lady you spoke of in your letters that I'm eagerly looking forward to that letter she is going to write.* Speaking of letters, I guess Eleanore has forgotten all about me. I haven't heard from her in over a month now, but with all the work she no doubt had to do before leaving on her vacation, she probably couldn't find the time. Seems funny- letters really don't take very long to write as a rule, but there are lots of times when you can't get away for a little while. At least that's the way it is with me.

You asked about fruit. Well, about all I can say to that is if oranges and bananas were dollar bills we

84

would all be millionaires. There is plenty of fruit of all kinds all the time and we get all we want. Matter of fact- We haven't missed anything yet except milk. It's been a long time since I last drank fresh milk. Can't even remember the last occasion. We can buy it, but it costs forty cents a quart and that's pretty steep.

Had a letter from home and they are getting along with that remodeling job at the lake. The big fellow has been classified 1-A. and is expecting his call most any time now. What a deal. The guy has to go thru two wars in one lifetime. I still think that's stretching things a bit too far.

Well Gang- Forgive me for rushing off so soon, but I've got a few more to write tonight and I want to get caught up if possible. I'll do better next time, I promise, so until then say "Hello" to everyone for me and write soon.

As ever,
Joe

You might tell Grandma that I caught up on my five hundred game while in the hospital and right now I'm just as sharp as a razor. Sure would like to sit in on a game one of these days soon.

J

*Or could this "young lady" be my mother? As I mentioned before, the rumor always was that my parents met after writing to each other during the war.
Mary Jo

Saturday November 14, 1942

Hello Gang,

Your letter arrived yesterday, but as it caught me smack in the middle of a twenty-five-mile hike, I haven't been able to do much about answering until tonight. After spending almost three weeks in the hospital I thought all that walking would get the best of me, but I guess I'm just a bit harder than I thought I was. I came thru in swell shape, not as much as a blister to show for all that walking. It's getting so I don't think any more of walking twenty-five miles than I used to think of walking for a paper.

Well, it's happened already. By the time you get this letter, the big fellow will be back in uniform getting in shape to fight his second war of his lifetime. I had a letter from home along with yours, and he will be in the army by the time this letter gets to you unless he is turned down at the induction board. I don't think there is much chance of that happening. They don't turn very many down once they get that far.

I'm sorry I made no mention of pictures last time I wrote. I forgot about it until after the letter was mailed and since it wasn't of much importance, I just let it keep until this letter. Yes- we've taken a lot of pictures and some of them should be coming back most any day now. Don't get too impatient, as it may be a few weeks before I can send them. Things are still touch and go with this G.I. soldier and will be for the rest of the month on account of missing payday.

While on the subject of pay and pictures, I've been giving lots of thought to Christmas and sending presents. As you know, it's rather hard for us to buy things and get them shipped, especially since I'll have to wait until after the first of next month to do my shopping. I have just about made up my mind to have some good portraits taken and send them for presents. They will go airmail with no trouble and it seems like a simple solution to a tough problem. What do you think of getting a picture of this mug of mine under the guise of a present?

As for your suggestion as to what I could use for Christmas. If you will be so kind as to wrap up a little cuddly blonde and send her airmail, I promise you she will be gratefully received. Seriously tho, there isn't much I can use out here. We are issued everything we really need (except the aforementioned blonde). And if you're going to send something I'm going to put it back in your lap and let you think of it. Be sure to get the postal regulations. I understand there are certain rules to be observed when shipping packages to foreign countries.

I had a letter from Eleanore today. Now that she has written and explained, I think I know what was wrong. I would say that my last letter to her was lost, because she certainly didn't get it. She had a grand time in Florida, as you no doubt have heard by now. I'll have to write to her tomorrow and swap stories about the land of oranges.

I was sorry to hear that Baldy is ailing. He has all my sympathy. That lying around in bed isn't what it's cracked up to be. Funny thing, this human nature, when you have to get up you wish you could stay in bed and vice-versa.

Rather a coincidence your writing me about going bowling. I was going to write you the same news. They have some alleys in one of the club houses near the port and we went over to try our luck several nights last week. I bowled about fifteen lines all told and my high was 196, my low 102, nuff said. We formed a team here in the company and we're hoping to get into a strictly G.I. tournament one of these days soon. Haven't heard anything further since we entered, but we are hoping for the best.

Well gang- it's getting late and the mail clerk will be gathering the letters soon so I had better close for now. Say "Hello" to everyone for me and write soon.

As ever,
Joe

Saw lots of swell shows this week. Gable and Turner in "Somewhere I'll Find You," Barbara Stanwyck in "The Gay Sisters" and Bing Crosby and Fred Astaire in "Holiday Inn." Don't miss any of them, they're all tops.

Wednesday, November 18, 1942

Hello Gang,

Got your swell letter yesterday and it sure was good hearing from you again. Had one from home along with yours and in some respects, they were identical. I mean the picture in the paper. Hardly think it does me justice, eyebrows and all, but at any rate, I can go off and get myself killed knowing that my picture was in the paper.

Sure sorry to hear that Baldy is still ailing. I hope this letter finds him as good as new.

Since I haven't heard anything to the contrary, I guess the big fellow is once again in the army. He wrote me last week saying he was notified to report for induction on Monday the 16th. I haven't heard as yet whether he was rejected, but I hardly think anything like that happened.

Have you heard from Brownie yet? I haven't heard a word, but I'm not really expecting to.

That was rather a nice picture you sent along. The old man sure done himself proud. And speaking of pappy, he is certainly looking good these days. He is one of those faces that is ageless. What a gentleman farmer he would make.

Last letter from home tells me that the remodeling on the summer home is completed. They say the place is so changed as to be almost unrecognizable what with the house being raised, the entire basement dug out and rebuilt, and last but not least a veranda, where the front porch and stairs used to be. They are planning to do some landscaping in the spring if conditions permit and when that's done, it should really be something.

I believe I told you last letter that I had heard from Eleanore and that the little misunderstanding we had has finally been straightened out. She made no mention when she wrote that she was planning to be in Chicago for the holidays. That girl is doing more travelling these days than FDR. That trip to Chicago for the holidays is one that this little GI wouldn't mind having a part of, but that's as far off for me as a trip to the moon would be.

I see we are back on the subject of Christmas presents again. Well, that blonde is still the best thing I can think of, so use your own judgment.

I haven't heard any comments about the weather lately. How has it been behaving itself? Must be pretty snippy these days. I guess maybe it's best I'm not around Chicago, as I would probably freeze to death inside of a day.

Well gang, I'm running out of words, so I guess I'll say goodbye until later. Give my regards to everyone for me and write soon.

As Ever,
Joe

What's with those big bad Bears?* Looks like they are so far in front of the rest of the field that the competition is practically nil. Since I'm the only one from Chicago in the company, it gives me a bang to bring up the Bears every time somebody starts to crow about the football in their section of the country. I haven't lost an argument yet.

*The Chicago Bears had an 11-0 season in 1942 under Head Coach George Halas.

90

Sunday November 30, 1942

Hello Gang,

   Here I am again, apology and all. I'm sorry that I've been unable to write sooner, but this is the first chance I've had since your letter arrived. I guess it will be like this from now on. Whatever writing I do will have to be done on Sundays, just as you do all of your writing on Fridays. We have been going at a plenty fast pace this week and if anything, it will get even faster in the weeks to come. I wish I could tell you of some of the things we are up to these days. Everything else we've done so far is dull by comparison. What stories there will be to tell you when I get back- assuming of course that I do get back and those odds are dropping fast.

   I had a letter from the block committee the other day.* The committee is the result of some deep thinking by one of the good neighbors. The idea of the whole thing is that they are going to keep in touch with all the boys in service who formerly lived on the block. There are eighteen of us all told and wouldn't you know that of the whole gang I am the only one out of the U.S. so far. Anyway, they wrote me a nice letter telling me of all the latest happenings in the neighborhood, and that they were sending me a box for Christmas. A sort of a community donation. Oh well, all gifts cheerfully received.

   I hardly think this will be any news to you, but the big fellow is finally and definitely in the army now. He passed his final exams and then took the two weeks furlough that all the new men are being given these days. He is leaving for Camp Grant tomorrow morning and from there who knows.

91

How are the boys getting along with their draft boards? I guess they will be called up most any time now.

What sort of a Thanksgiving did you have? A good time was had by all I hope. We had a nice turkey dinner with all the fixings, but we had a good day's work to get up an appetite. As it looks now, our Christmas and New Year's won't be a bit different from last year's. Remember? I hope this old war comes to an end in time for us to get home next year.

Listened to the Ohio State- Iowa pre-flight game yesterday and it was a honey. If we could only bring in one of the Bears' games, life would be complete.

Everybody seems to have the same idea about Christmas presents that you had. So far four people have asked me to tell them what I want for a gift. If they all send me the blonde I asked for, I don't know what I'm going to do with all the women. Start a harem or something.

Well gang- I don't expect to have any more time for writing this week so I had better close for now and try answering a few more before bedtime. Say "Hello" to everyone for me and write soon.

As Ever,
Joe

Tell Baldy to get himself in shape soon.

*During World War II, Chicago neighborhoods organized an extensive network to support the war effort. 27,000 elected block captains oversaw ceremonies to honor their neighbors who were leaving to serve and built shrines to remember those who didn't return. By war's end, the average Chicago block had seven residents serving in the military.

Bushmaster Snake
(Courtesy of Arizona State University Library)

Jungle Training
(Courtesy of Arizona State University Library)

Camp Theater in Panama
(Courtesy of Arizona State University Library)

Bushmaster Bowl
(Courtesy of Arizona State University Library)

Bushmaster Flag
(Courtesy of Arizona State University Library)

Bushmaster Snake and Machete Logo Adopted in Panama

Meanwhile, in New Guinea and the Philippines, the stage was being set for future Bushmaster Operations

Timeline of 1942 South Pacific

January 2, 1942
Japanese forces enter and occupy Manila.

January 7-23, 1942
80,000 U.S. and Philippine troops are forced to pull back from Japanese offenses in the Philippines.

January 11, 1942
The Japanese advance through Malaya continues.

January 20, 1942
Japanese begin air bombardment on Rabaul, New Britain.

February 6, 1942
U.S. forces advance on Luzon, Philippines, but make little progress against Japanese forces

March 8, 1942
The battle for New Guinea begins as the Japanese land at Lae and Salumaua in the Huon Gulf.

March 10, 1942
Japanese holdings in New Guinea strengthen when troops land at Finschhafen.

March 12, 1942
General MacArthur leaves the Bataan Peninsula in the Philippines with his famous parting words: "I shall return."

March 14, 1942
U.S. troops begin to arrive in Australia in order to prepare for invasions of New Guinea and elsewhere.

April 1, 1942
Japanese troops land in Hollandia on the north coast of New Guinea and Sorong on the west coast.

April 5-7, 1942
Japanese inflict heavy casualties upon the U.S. in Bataan, Philippines; forcing the Americans to retreat.

April 6, 1942
Japanese land at Bouganville in the Solomon Islands. They also occupy Buka Island in the Solomons.

April 8, 1942
 U.S. soldiers in the Philippines are ordered to destroy their artillery in order to prepare for surrender to the Japanese.

April 9, 1942
Remaining U.S. forces surrender to the Japanese in the Philippines. 78,000 U.S. and Philippine troops are made to walk 65 miles in terrible conditions by their captors. 1 out of 3 men die on what later became known as the Bataan Death March.

April 10, 1942
U.S. Pacific Fleet reorganizes.

April 30, 1942
U.S. troops officially withdraw from Buna.

May 6, 1942
Corregidor, off the coast of the Bataan Peninsula, falls to the Japanese.

May 9, 1942
The Battle of the Coral Sea helps stop Japanese expansion in Papua, New Guinea and the Solomon Islands.

May 10, 1942
U.S. officially surrenders in the Philippines. 12,550 U.S. and Philippine soldiers become prisoners of the Japanese.

June 3, 1942
Battle of the Midway begins. The Japanese are focused on taking the Aleutian Islands and the important military air base on Midway Island.

June 5, 1942
After two days of heavy fighting, the Battle of the Midway ends with the Japanese losing half of their carrier fleet and 275 aircraft. This U.S. victory is a turning point in the Pacific Theatre.

July 7-12, 1942
Australian troops take a five-day march across the Owen Stanley Mountains in Papua, New Guinea in order to take up defensive positions on the Kokoda Trail.

August 7, 1942
The First Marine Division lands on Guadalcanal in the Solomon Islands. This is the first major U.S. offensive in the war, and is aimed at securing Henderson Airfield.

August 8, 1942
Henderson Airfield is secured by U.S. forces.

August 8-11, 1942
Kokoda Trail is temporarily recaptured by Australian and Papuan troops, however, after three days, they are forced back to Port Moresby.

August 18-20, 1942
Japanese attacks are repulsed in Guadalcanal.

August 25-26, 1942
Milne Bay, New Guinea is invaded by a small unit of 1200 Japanese soldiers. This landing is resisted by Australian troops.

September 3-7, 1942
Japanese reinforcements land in Buna, New Guinea.

September 12-14, 1942
Japanese 25th Brigade begins an assault on Henderson Airfield. U.S. Marines engage in a two-day battle which ends with Japanese withdrawal.

November 11-13, 1942
Australian troops successfully push back the Japanese on the Kokoda Trail; ensuring the safety of Port Moresby.

December 9, 1942
U.S. forces on Guadalcanal reach 58,000. The Japanese are losing strength with 20,000 poorly equipped troops remaining.

PART III
AUSTRALIA
1943

*"I'm in Australia and having the time of my
not so young life."*

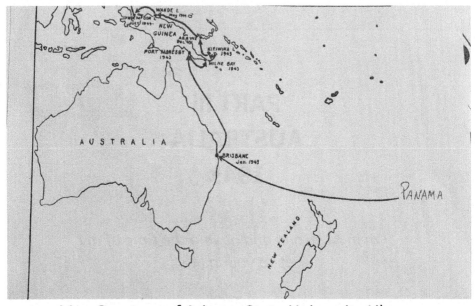

Map Courtesy of Arizona State University Library

The Bushmasters spent one hard year in Panama: clearing jungles, building camps, loading and unloading trucks and ships, testing equipment, patrolling the outer defenses of the Panama Canal and taking part in espionage. But most of all, they prepared to fight a ruthless enemy in an unimaginable environment.

When the Bushmasters left Panama, they suspected they were headed for New Guinea. They were half-right. New Guinea was in their future, but not before they enjoyed a well-earned rest in Australia.

In late January 1943, after a three-week journey, they arrived in Brisbane, Australia. Initially, they stayed at the Doomben Racetrack, which was closed in order to host Allied troops passing through. The Bushmasters enjoyed three weeks of good food and the hospitality of the Democratic Australians.

It's obvious that Joe was too busy enjoying himself to write, as evidenced by his single letter.

Hello Gang,

I've just a few moments to spare, but it's been so long since I last wrote to you and may be longer before I write again, that I'm going to finish regardless of who calls. Your letter arrived yesterday and it was so good hearing from you again. There must be an awfully big difference in the mail service from here in Australia, because I've had only four letters since coming down here. It always works that way when we change our address.

I gather from your last letter that at the time you wrote, you still hadn't received my last one saying where I am. Well, I'm still in Australia and having the time of my not so young life. Now that I've mastered the value of the money and can understand the King's English, this is really the life. I've never seen so many good-looking women gathered in one place before. They could give the girls back home all the competition in the world. They're that nice.

Sorry to hear that Frank is still not well. I find it hard to believe that Baldy could be in such a condition. As long as I've known him, he has had only a few bad days and all this being sick must have him fit to be tied. Tell him to keep punching.

Haven't heard a thing from El since coming down here, but she will get around to writing one of these fine days. She always does.

Well Gang, there is lots more to write about and if it's at all possible, I will write more tomorrow or the next day. I would like to tell you all about the country and city life, but I'm not certain just how much of it would get through.

Give my best to everyone and write often. More often than I do.

Love to all,
Joe

PART IV
New Guinea
and New Britain
1943-1944

"I had an idea that we had served our hitch in hell, but compared to this place it was a Sunday school picnic."

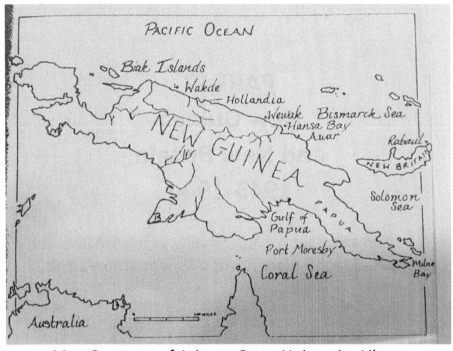

Map Courtesy of Arizona State University Library

Early February 1943 marked the fifteenth month of the war with Japan. The next stop for The Bushmasters was New Guinea. The New Guinea Operation was divided into five phases. Phase 1, the Japanese occupation of New Guinea, was well underway. Japan had been able to tear through Southeast Asia, expanding their territory and power. The United States had had a presence in the Philippines for decades, and yet, Japan was able to take control of the Philippines in four months' time. They had also captured Hong Kong, Singapore and Malaya, and had pushed the British army out of Burma. New Guinea was almost totally in their control by mid-1942. New Guinea possessed much needed natural resources, as well as a prime location for the Japanese to protect their military supply lines. They also fortified the northern coast of New Guinea with bases and airstrips. The U.S. advance on Buna in November 1942 came with a victory in January 1943. This was the beginning of a long struggle to gain a foothold in New Guinea.

New Guinea is a large island that stretches 1500 miles from east to west and lies to the north of Australia and to the southeast of the Philippines. Phase 2 involved the Japanese attempt to capture the U.S. holdings in southern New Guinea. The Japanese already occupied the northeastern part of New Guinea. They had captured the northern coastal towns of Finschhafen, Lae, and Salamaua in order to prepare for a seaborne attack on Port Moresby. Port Moresby, located in the southwestern part of New Guinea, along with Milne Bay was still under the control of the U.S. and Allied forces. This port was vital to maintain, because it was within air striking and invasion distance to Australia. It was also the only port in New Guinea supporting Allied operations. If Japan could take Port Moresby, they would not only be a direct threat to Australia, but be capable of disrupting Allied supply and communication lines. This would have been a turning point in favor of Japan. MacArthur was determined to protect Port Moresby and then begin to drive the Japanese forces out of New Guinea.

MacArthur called for more troops to come to New Guinea. Facilities were inadequate to support the number of soldiers that would be moving through. These facilities had to be developed at the same time that troops were moving into position. Combat battalions, like the 158th, were worked to the point of exhaustion. In their downtime from battle, instead of resting and recuperating, they were building facilities for future operations.

In the meantime, Japanese Naval losses at both the Battle of the Midway and the battle of the Coral Sea stalled their attack by sea on Port Moresby. Determined and ruthless, the Japanese walked the Kokoda Trail, a stretch of impassable jungle in the Owen-Stanley mountain range that would take them to Port Moresby. At one point, it was estimated that there were 14,000 Japanese soldiers on the trail getting more than halfway to their target. Fearlessly, they pushed the Australian army back through the most difficult terrain. The American attack on Guadalcanal finally affected this group, because the Japanese were forced to stall the operation in order to defend Guadalcanal. The Japanese soldiers who were left behind died of starvation on the Kokoda Trail, and Port Moresby remained under Allied command.

The Japanese defenses were weakening as U.S. offenses were strengthening. In spite of this, Japan had some distinct advantages over the U.S. forces. Fighting the war on two fronts was challenging the U.S. Records show that the United States engaged roughly 80% of her military power in the European fight against Hitler. The Pacific Theatre had to make do with the remaining 20%. Japan's other advantage was the Japanese soldier's willingness to die for the Imperial Empire. It was considered an honor to die fighting and a dishonor to surrender. This gave the Japanese the ability to be treacherous and ferocious without any fear, thus creating a great psychological advantage.

Phase 3 was the American offensive aimed at Japanese operations in Rabaul, New Britain, an island located next to the mainland of New Guinea. MacArthur and his staff considered Rabaul, located on the northeastern tip of New Britain, as the cornerstone of the Japanese outer defenses. Heavily fortified with an underground network of tunnels, Rabaul also held 100,000 soldiers just waiting for an attack by the Allies. Direct attack on Rabaul may have been certain suicide. MacArthur decided that attacking the less defended Arawe and Gasmata would allow better access to Rabaul. Operation Cartwheel began the summer of 1943. Its objective was to encircle Rabaul, isolating it from the other Japanese positions. MacArthur's troops advanced toward Rabaul from the southeast.

Simultaneously, Admiral Halsey was advancing north through the Solomon Islands in order to complete the isolation.

The Bushmasters played a large part in capturing Arawe six months after Operation Cartwheel began. Three months later, in March 1944, Rabaul was neutralized. The Japanese mainland was isolated from needed resources, such as oil and rubber. This was a good start for MacArthur's goal, but conquest in New Guinea was far from accomplished. Recapturing New Guinea was vital to stopping the Japanese advancement in the Pacific.

The story of the 158th Regimental Combat Team had just begun. The next few months would test their readiness for jungle warfare.

Timeline of the 158th Regimental Combat Team
February-April 1943

February 1943
Bushmasters set sail from Australia headed for New Guinea. The wine, women, and song are just a memory. Hopefully, these sweet memories will sustain them for a while, because there are rough times ahead.

March 1943
Bushmasters arrive in Port Moresby, New Guinea. The 32nd and 41st Infantry Divisions are already there after the recent bloody battles for the recapture of Buna, Gona, Lae, and Sananada. They all remain busy with coastal defenses and constructing Camp Carlew.

Joe's letters resume on March 27, 1943.

April-December 1943
The Bushmasters move on to Milne Bay where they prepare for an offensive and build another camp. Later, this camp becomes known as the biggest installation in the Pacific. They also receive training on new beach landing craft not yet used in combat. The headquarters of General Walter Krueger's Sixth Army is established on Milne Bay in June 1943. The 2nd Battalion, of which Joe is a member, is assigned to be the security force for the General.
The Bushmasters are split up and go three different ways: Kiriwana, Woodlark, and Goodenough Island. The 2nd Battalion continues to guard the General, following a headquarters move to Goodenough Island, where there is an airbase. The 1st and 3rd Battalions on Kiriwana and Woodlark Islands continued cutting jungle and building airstrips and camps.

March 27, 1943 (presumably Port Moresby)
Hello Gang,

  Good thing these V letters don't have too much
writing space, because I've got just enough time to fill
this page. This is the first chance I've had to write
letters for almost a month now, and I've got more to
write then I can count up to. I'm still waiting for a
letter from you- in fact a letter from anybody. The
mail sure has slowed up considerably since we left our
last home. Used to think it was bad there, but now it
takes a letter two months to get here.

  Well, going to Australia sure was swell while it
lasted. The only thing wrong with the idea was that it
didn't last long enough. Just as we were really getting
solid with all those sweet Aussie gals came some more
moving orders and I am now in New Guinea. I used
to think that hell hole we came from was bad, but I'm
ready to admit it was a picnic compared to this place.
I was curious to see a Fuzzy Wuzzy,* but now that I've
seen one, I'm ready to leave at any time. Looks like
the luck will have to be riding high if a guy's to be
leaving here at all tho.

  Had a weekend pass just before we left. (the first one
in almost sixteen months) and I've at least got some
sweet memories. Not half enough of them though.

113

Have the boys heard anything new from their draft board? How is Frank getting along? Much better I hope. Well, I'm about out of space so I will close for now and try to write again in a day or two. Say "Hello" to everyone for me and write soon. Regards to all.

As ever,
Joe

*Slang term for New Guinea native coined by British colonial soldiers

Hi Gang,

It certainly was swell to hear from you again in so short a time. Either the mail service is getting better or time is passing faster than ever before, but the mailman has certainly been good to me this week.

Sort of curious about that date I had, aren't you? With writing space being so scarce I can't go into all of the details, but it wasn't anything unusual. That is-it wouldn't be unusual back home, but after that year in the jungles, it was as tho from heaven. About all we did was go to the show, and to the dances with the usual excursions to the restaurants.

You have probably had my letter by now telling you that we are on New Guinea, so even that brief vacation we had in Australia is nothing but a memory. Speaking of New Guinea, I had an idea that we had served our hitch in hell, but compared to this place it was a Sunday school picnic. This is really the hellhole of them all.

Frank has received his classification? Has his health improved to where the army will take him? I guess it won't be long before John gets his call now. Oh well, no life like the army life. Especially when you have no choice. Had a letter from the big fellow the other day, and he is now in California and not liking it too much. He should get out while the getting is good.

Well gang- Here I am at the end of the allotted space again so I'll start to say Goodbye until next time. Say "Hello" to all for me and tell Grandma to take good care of herself, because when I get back and start winning at 500, I don't want any alibis. Write soon.

As Ever,
Joe

April 10, 1943 (presumably Milne Bay)
Hello Gang,

Yes, the mail service certainly has improved since we first got down here. Your letters are starting to come as regular as clockwork, and I for one am tickled pink. Getting a letter that contains news is just like listening to a radio or reading a newspaper out here. Haven't seen either a radio or newspaper for so long now that it's all I can do to remember what they look like or what purpose they serve.

So, Frank is feeling better these days? I was glad to hear that he is back to normal again. I always had a hard time of it picturing him as nervous and generally run down. The only time I have ever seen him ailing was when he was operated on and I guess that was the reason. I suppose he will be going into the army most any day now. I guess they don't lose any time about those things anymore. I still think it would be a good idea for him to enlist in the Air Corps.

I think I told you in my last letter that the big fellow is about to get a discharge because of his age. I had a letter from him the other day and he says he is going to try and get a job in California when he gets out. He will probably last for a month or two and come running back to Chicago.

Well Gang, here I am at the end of the space again, so I will close until later. Say "Hello" to all for me and wish Grandma a belated happy birthday for me. Also offer my congratulations to Joy and Janet should you see them. What a name. What a name. Well bye again.

As ever,
Joe

.4, 1943

Gang,

is letter is being written on an impulse. Suddenly found myself with a few hours of idle time on my hands, and since it's been almost a week now since I last wrote to you, I thought it would be a good idea to take pen in hand and get busy. Have been expecting a letter from you the last couple of days, but no luck as yet. Maybe this afternoon's mail call will bring some good news.

I think that I could make a letter sound fairly interesting if it weren't for that censor man, because he doesn't leave a guy too much to talk about. The things that have happened, what a job it's going to be, trying to recall all of them when I get back. Assuming that I do get back and I'm a bit doubtful about that.

Well, tomorrow being Easter, I suppose you are busy as bees getting everything in shape, coloring eggs and what have you. I'm going to church in the morning and that will be the extent of the holiday as far as I'm concerned. Haven't seen a fresh egg for so long now there's no reason to expect any changes in the diet because of Easter. What I wouldn't give for a couple of pork chops and eggs.

How are the Cubs and Sox doing? Or have they called baseball off for the duration?* What little news we do get is generally about two months old, so we are not exactly up on things. Well, I'll have to close for now. Will write again in a day or two and until then I'll say "Hello" to all and .....be good.

As ever,
Joe

*There was much discussion as to whether Major League Baseball should be suspended for the duration of the war. The league had lost many star players, such as Ted Williams, Stan Musial, Joe DiMaggio, and Yogi Berra to enlistment. In his Green Light Letter, President Roosevelt wrote "I honestly feel that it would be best for the country to keep baseball going. There will be fewer people unemployed and everybody will work longer hours and harder than ever before. And that seems that they ought to have a chance for recreation and for taking their minds off their work even more than before."

The minor leagues lost even greater numbers of players to the military, thus opening the door to The All-American Girls Professional Ball League.

1943

ohn and Lou,

r ever-welcome letter arrived yesterday and it was a pleasure to hear from you again so soon. I guess the letters from home do more to keep a guy from cracking up than anything else. At least that is the way I feel about it. Surprising- the way a letter comes along just when you get to thinking that nothing matters anymore and gives you that needed lift and take it from me, you do need a lift in this part of the world.

Give my apologies to El and I do owe her a letter, but have been unable to write because of no address. Tell her to drop me a line and I promise not to fall behind again.

Glad to hear that you are once again climbing the ladder of success Lou, knowing what a glutton for work you are. Keep up the good work.

Glad to hear that they finally decided to open the major league season. Last time I saw a paper there seemed to be some doubt as to whether they would play anymore for the duration. Let me know how the Cubs and Sox are making out from time to time-will you?

Well gang-something's just come up and I'll have to run. Say "Hello" to everyone for me and write soon.

As ever,
Joe

Am still feeling like a million and hoping this letter finds all of you the same.

May 26, 1943

Hello Gang,

Again, I'll have to ask your forgiveness for not writing sooner. It's the same old story - so damn busy. Your letter written on the 8th was received yesterday and as always it was so good hearing from you, although I'm afraid my answer to it may be somewhat disappointing. In one of my recent letters to the folks, I asked them to send me some news on a rumor we had heard- the one about Congress passing a law that no one would be kept overseas for more than twenty months. I probably worded it in such a way as to mislead them into thinking I was about to get a furlough. Well- I sure wish it were true, but as far as I know, we are as far from that as ever. Of course, we have been overseas for a year and a half now and it's just possible that we may be coming back to the States one of these months soon, but I'm not planning on it yet. I'll let you know when and if anything definite turns up and in the meantime, the best way of getting home in a hurry is to get this war won.

Did you give El my message? Have been looking forward to a letter from her, but no luck yet.

I understand it's once again permissible to send small packages overseas. If true, I wonder if you would send along a couple of decks of cards? They are impossible to buy here and they are about our only means of recreation. I've asked the folks to send some too, but a few extra packs would be more than welcome. Well gang- I see I'm about out of space so I'll close until later. I'm still as well as ever and am hoping this letter finds all of you the same.

Say "Hello" to all for me.   As Ever, Joe

June 5, 1943
New Guinea
Hello Gang-

Your letter of the 15th of May arrived yesterday and as always it was so good hearing from you. A rather unusual thing happened. I had a letter from home along with yours-written on the 17th and they told me that John had stopped over and told them that both he and Frank had been called up for their tests. I gather that Frank must have been notified after you wrote. Since it takes almost three weeks for a letter to get here, I guess that one or maybe both of the boys have been inducted already. Pretty rough deal. I think this, because this business is fast coming to a close, and it won't be too much longer before we are all back again drinking beer and playing pinochle-I hope.

Wrote to Eleanore yesterday at long last. I'll bet she's having kittens about my speed in writing to her.

One of the boys went on a trek into the jungles yesterday and of all things-came back with a hog. He paid a pound and a half for it. About 5 bucks, and since it weighed about 200, you would have to call it a bargain. The fresh meat will be a welcome relief to all of us.

Well gang- space is about gone, so I'll say goodbye until next time. Say "Hello" to all for me and write soon.

Love to all,
Joe

John must have the weather situation all figured out.

June 15, 1943

Hello Gang,

Had some good luck in today's mail call. Found five letters waiting for me, including two from you and even tho it might be taking advantage of you, this answering two of your letters with one- that's what I'm going to do.

Sorry to hear that Grandma is ailing again. Tell her to take good care of herself for me.

Had a very nice letter from Milly the other day. She told me all about the "I Am an American Day" * that was held in Soldier Field and with her flair for telling things-what a treat.

Last letter from the folks said that John had told them that Brownie was doing some fighting in Africa. Have you heard from him lately?

Sure would like to trade some of this jungle fighting for some of that desert stuff. I figure it's about four times as simple.

Also heard that you've been having practice blackouts and air-raid alerts. Not likely that Chicago will ever have the real thing, but it's a good idea to be prepared. If nothing else, the subway should make good bomb shelters. I can remember a few times when I wished it was next to me rather than the old hole in the ground.

Well children, I see I'm at the end again so I'll say goodbye until later. I was only kidding at the start- I'll write again in a day or two. Say "Hello" to all for me and write soon.

As ever,
Joe

*President Roosevelt designated Sunday, May 18th, 1941 as the first "I Am an American" Day in order to recognize those who attained citizenship status.

June 22, 1943

Hello Gang,

Received your ever-welcome letter yesterday, and as always it was swell hearing from you.

Had a pleasant surprise today in the form of a letter from Janet. She rebuked my remarks about her new offspring in a mild sort of manner, but I don't think she was serious. Will try to answer in a day or two with a few more well-chosen remarks. She told me of a dream she had recently in which I played the part of her third husband. I'll bet I didn't make a very good husband this far away. Speaking of dreams, I dreamt that I was wed to two women at the same time. I had a pretty good time of it, but I'm wondering if all these weddings make me a trigamist.

Had a long-delayed letter from Milly yesterday. The V-mail* was damaged and couldn't be photographed. as a result, it has been on the way since May tenth.

Well Gang. I'll say so long until later. Say "Hello" to all for me and write soon.

As ever,
Joe

*V-mail is short for Victory Mail. It was used during World War II to speed up mail service for armed forces in combat zones. The process involved writing on small letter sheets that were photographed and sent to their destination on microfilm to be printed before delivery.

July 3, 1943

Hi Gang,

Seems a long time between letters this trip. Actually, it was no longer than usual, but I was looking forward to hearing from you and, of course, doing that always makes time drag. Why was I looking forward? I really don't know - just something I can't define. Anyway, I was glad to hear that everything is going along alright.

Well. Tomorrow's that noisy day again.* I don't suppose you have made any plans to speak of - just a day of rest. Did they sell fireworks this year? I suppose not. We will probably spend the holiday in much the same way we have spent all our holidays recently. I don't doubt that we will have our share of fireworks. Speaking of fireworks again, your papers must be telling you lots of them from out this way. Never a dull moment and what a life.

Looks like my faith in the Sox is going to be rewarded this year. At least to the extent of beating thou gorgeous Cubs.

Well Gang - I have to say goodbye for now. Will try to write again soon. In the meantime say "Hello" to everyone for me and write soon.....

Love to all,
Joe

*The 4th of July was observed in the United States during World War II. However, the focus of the day was on honoring those who were fighting to retain our independence.

July 12, 1943

Hello Gang,

The surprise and shock of getting a letter written by John almost tempts me to answer him and him alone. Sure was nice hearing from him, but I suspect the fine hand of someone else in the writing. It just didn't sound like John.

Thirty cents a shot for liquor does seem like a hell of a lot to pay, but I guess the way they are making money these days they can afford it. The price out here is six to seven pounds a quart (about 18-20 bucks) and even that price is not too much for the boys, except that there is none to be had so we just do without. Not even a bottle of beer.

Since Frank went up for his final on the third, I suppose he will be in the Army by the time this gets to you. I still think he should have enlisted in the Air Corps. Well Gang - will have to say so long until later. Give my best to everyone and write soon...

As ever,
Joe

July 19, 1943

Hello Gang,

I just have time for a few hasty lines, but it's been so long since I last wrote, I thought you might like to hear the news I can't tell you about. Sounds sort of contradictory doesn't it?

We haven't had a mail call in over a week now, so of course no letters. Should get all kinds of news when and if our mail catches up with us.

Have been as busy as a bee lately. Seems like the time just flies when you're working hard and that does help out here. Before you know it, the holidays will be here again and me further than ever from home. If any outfit in this man's army is due for a break, we're that outfit. So, I'm keeping my fingers crossed and hoping.

I suppose your next letter will tell me that Frank is in the army. Tell the boys to keep writing me when and if they are called in.

Well Gang- I'll say goodbye for now. Give my best to everyone and write soon...

As ever,
Joe

July 27, 1943

Hello Gang,

Had a very pleasant surprise yesterday. Finally had the overdue mail call and I found two letters from you. Sure was nice hearing from you and all the good news too. Glad to hear about Frank and sorry too. That must sound a little contradictory, but you know what I mean.

Had a letter from Annabelle. John and Frank will recall her telling me that she is married. I hadn't heard from her in almost a year, but I guess she just had to tell someone.

I wish now I had told you not to send pinochle cards and saved you some trouble. What we need are playing cards for our bridge games. Yes, I said bridge. We bought all the pinochle decks in the ship's store on the way down from Panama, and even after all this time it's still possible to find a few decks around.

I can understand what you mean about the heat back home. We are in the middle of a tropical heat wave (Imagine) and a cold snap would come in handy.

Well Gang- this is a poor excuse for a letter after so long a time, but I'll do better next time. Say "Hello" to all for me and write soon.

As ever,
Joe

August 8, 1943

Hello Gang,

I'm one jump ahead of you this time. Had a letter from Laura and so I know all about John's rejection. Well- maybe no details about the rejection.

What's the secret of the boys' success? Must be a relief- having it all over and done with. Makes it easier to plan the future.

Have been hearing quite regularly from Janet. She sends me letters in the form of news bulletins. And I'm practically a walking encyclopedia on current events. Heard the other day that my Sox are in second place. Any truth in the rumor?

Well. Four more days and I pass another milestone in life. If this keeps up much longer, I'll be old and gray when I do get back. Shouldn't complain tho. Getting back old and gray will be better than not getting back at all.

We're looking forward to seeing a show tonite- "Her Cardboard Lover." Oh well, what can you expect way off the beaten path. I'll say goodbye now. Give my best to all and write soon........

As ever,
Joe

August 12, 1943 (Joe's birthday)
Hello Gang,

Received your ever-welcome letter yesterday and as always, it was good hearing from you. As I told you last letter, the news of John's deferment was no news and as for feeling bad about it, what can a guy do.

Am spending my 29th milestone today in the dullest way imaginable. Just the same old routine. Come to think about it - if this war don't hurry up and get over and done with I'll be as old as sin when I get back. Looking back, it doesn't seem half as long as it's been. Do you realize that in a short time it will be three Christmases away from home?

Have been hearing some rumors on the doings of my White Sox. Is it true they're in second place?

I am looking forward to getting the pics you spoke of. When you get ready to send them - regular letters sent air mail get here just as fast as Vmail.

Well Gang - I see I'm about out of space again so I'll say Goodbye until next time. I am still well and hoping that this letter finds all of you the same. Give my best to everyone and write soon.....

As ever,
Joe

August 23, 1943

Hello Gang,

Had two very nice letters yesterday and both of them from you. The mailman has been playing hard to get this last week, so they were doubly appreciated.

Still haven't received the cards, but I've learned not to be impatient with the boat mail. They will get here one of these fine days. I did receive two magazines ("American", "Redbook") that I subscribed to about six months ago and that has been some help. The picture situation has been taken care of and we could look forward to one show a week from now on. All in all, things have progressed to a point where it's not bad at all. Course, we're still without hot and cold running water, steaks and chickens, but it's not bad. I would like to see a few bright lights and hear some good music again, but that is still somewhere in the future.

Well gang- I'll have to close for now. Say "Hello" to all and write soon-

As ever,
Joe

September 5, 1943

Hello Gang,

Forgive me for being so long in answering, but there has been a temporary shortage of these V-mail blanks, so I could do nothing but wait. To top it off I had quite a few letters the other day and I'm having to spend every minute of my spare time in trying to catch up.

Had a letter from the big fella and he has graduated as a full-fledged radio operator and mechanic on the Flying Forts.* He's doing plenty of flying and apparently enjoying it. Says he may be sent overseas.

I hear you are having your share of heat this year. Can't say that I envy you, but I would like to look forward to some cool fall days. It looks now as if that will have to wait for the duration. Guess we are doomed to stay here until then. There is a small chance of my going on furlough to Australia for seven short days soon. I'm keeping my fingers crossed. Well, bye for now. Say "Hello" to all and write soon.

As Ever,
Joe

*The Flying Forts refers to the Boeing B17 heavy bomber known as The Flying Fortress.

September 15, 1943

Hello Gang,

Have two letters from you that need answering, but will have time for only one of them today. I can remember when the mail calls were more regular and answering letters wasn't half as difficult. Seems like every time I have mail, there are six letters and it takes me a week to catch up.

Had a letter from Janet yesterday written from New York. Says she's having a marvelous time. She writes a nice letter, but aren't you being just a bit modest Lou? Wish I could say as much as you do on just one page. The idea of going on furlough has occurred to me too. It's possible that I may get to go back to Australia for a week sometime in the near future, but that is the very best I'm hoping for. It would help some tho.

Well gang. I see I've used all the space and said next to nothing. I'll say Goodbye now and write again in a few days. Give my best to everyone and write soon.......

As ever,
Joe

September 20, 1943

Hello Gang,

Received your ever-welcome letter yesterday and as always it was good hearing from you. Brownie's address was a pleasant surprise- I had given up on the guy a long time ago, but now that I know where he is, I'll drop him a line. You're quite right: he has covered lots of territory since leaving the States. With him in the European Theatre and me in the Southwest Pacific, you guys are going to get plenty of first hand and plenty of bull...on how this war was won when we get back.

We had another one of our infrequent movies last night. This time "The Mayor of 44th Street" and Gene Autry in "Capistrano" something or other. Not much, but sure did look good to us. I haven't heard any more in regards to that short leave in Australia, but am still hoping for the best. Will say goodbye for now. Give my best to all and write soon......

As ever,
Joe

September 29, 1943

Hello Gang,

Seems a long time since I last heard from you. I looked back through my letters just for curiosity's sake, and it really has been just over a week between letters, so it must be that time is passing more slowly than usual. Things have been a little quiet this week- nothing much doing beyond the routine stuff that goes on all the time and the peace and quiet has been welcome.

Have been hearing some good things about The Bears. Looks like they will be the team to beat again. I promoted myself into a ten pound ($32) bet on the World Series the other day. Don't know enough about any team this year to do any gambling on them, but I think The Yankees would make a good bet at any time. Sure would like to hear a few of the games.

Had a letter from Joy and Janet the other day, and Janet tells me she had a good time on her trip. I asked for a report on the doings of Joy while the cat was away. Well guys, here is the end again. Give my best to everyone and don't be too long in writing....

As ever,
Joe

October 14, 1943
Hello Gang,

Once again, my apologies for being so long in answering, but it has been a busy week and none of us has had a moment to spare for anything. Your letter arrived several days ago and I enjoyed it very much, especially Lou's joining the company bowling team. I can make any number of remarks, but will restrain myself from saying any more than- What do you mean the low scoring was to be expected after not bowling for five years? I can recall many occasions within the last three and a half. Still, it makes a good argument.

What did you use for gas when you went on that fruit-picking junket?

I polished up quite a bundle on the Yanks World Series victory. Converted quite a few Cardinal fans at the same time. The only trouble is having no way of spending my ill-gotten gains.

Well guys- will have to close until later. I'm still in good health and hoping this letter finds all of you the same. Give my best to all and write soon...

As ever,
Joe

Had a nice letter from Brownie.

AEJ

October 20, 1943

Dear Lou,

Just time for a few words, but I wanted to get this ring in the mail and on its way as soon as possible.

It makes a nice souvenir and I hope you like it. It's made from part of a shot down Jap Zero and the setting is part of a shell we had the natives dive for. Wanted to send one to Kay, but haven't been able to bring one down to her size yet. Tell her I'm working on it and will do my best to get it to her as soon as possible. Haven't been able to do much good for the boys either, but I'm working on that too.

Will say bye for now and write you a V-mail in a few days. Say "Hello" to all and be good...

Love,
Joe

October 20, 1943

Hello Gang,

This makes the second letter to you today. The other will probably be sometime in getting to you, as it will have to travel by boat until it reaches the States. I sent a little something for Lou- the letter will tell all.

Had a letter from Laura the other day and all she talked about was her Al's going into the navy and that he was coming home on furlough. Is she really as depressed as all that? One would think he was expected to win the war single- handed and then get killed just as the Armistice was being signed.

If you were having this weather at home you would call it dog days. It's even warmer than usual and believe me, it's almost too much.

Had a show the other night-Bing Crosby in "Holiday Inn." I saw it in Panama, but enjoyed it all over again. That White Christmas business does make a guy feel homesick for a few minutes. Well guys, I'll have to close now. Say "Hello" to all and write soon...

As ever,
Joe

October 29, 1943

Hello Gang,

For seven long months now, we have been doing with an occasional movie and damn glad to get it and now all of a sudden, we are blossoming into sated movie goers. These last four nights have been hectic ones indeed. By doing a little hitch-hiking to other areas every night we have seen no less than three different pictures in as many days and last night we topped it off by going to a jam session at the quartermaster's company. They have some eight balls in that outfit that can really give out with that stuff. One of the boys used to make his living playing for Cab Calloway and another for Kate Waller, and what a treat to listen to them. I'm writing this under the influence of a slight hangover. Yes! We even managed that. It comes plenty high -ten pounds ($32) a quart, but there is no other way of spending it. Can you imagine spending $3.20 for a bottle of Dutch Ale. The guys that sell it will wind up with millions and we'll end up in the poorhouse. Well kids, I'll say a shaky goodbye and try writing again tomorrow when I'm a bit more balanced. Say "Hello" to all and write soon....

As ever
Joe

Sure wish I had some of that chicken you wrote about.
J

November 8, 1943

Hello Gang,

Found your letter waiting for me when I came in last nite and it was a fitting climax to a busy, but very interesting day. Being Sunday things were rather quiet and I spent the day reading, playing bridge, going to the show (The picture was "Standby For Action") and now, answering a few letters before hitting the hay. That might sound a bit complicated, but I was up all night working and it is now morning.

Had a nice letter from your mother the other day, Lou. It's been so long since she last wrote to me that I wasn't really expecting a letter, so it was a pleasant surprise. Also heard from El early this week, but she said nothing about the boyfriend you spoke of, so I am in the dark. What are the bloody details?

Well. I see I'm at the end of the page again. Think I'll put the other letters off until later and try getting some shuteye before it gets too hot.

Say "Hello" to everyone and write soon........

As ever,
Joe

November 18, 1943

Hello Gang,

It has been a long time since I last wrote to you, but I won't try to offer any excuse. It's bothered me - not being able to find the time for a letter, but there was nothing I could do about it. Received my second letter from you yesterday and will answer it in a day or two.

It's much the same here with me as it is with you. Plenty of news, but not much of it is writable. Your birthday cards by V-mail arrived the other day and I enjoyed them very much. There was no need of your apologizing about being late. I almost forgot about it myself. Birthdays and holidays have all but lost their meaning to us. They are just another day. I saw a menu for Thanksgiving the other day and it said Turkey. I don't know where it's coming from, but I hope they were right. Will give you the bloody details later.

Had a very nice letter from El yesterday telling me all about the Notre Dame-Army game. The Irish must have a powerhouse this year.

How are The Bears doing? Well kids, I am going to say bye again. Say "Hello" to all for me and I'll be waiting to hear from you.......

Love,
Joe

November 24, 1943
Hello Gang,

I suppose I should have put this letter off until tomorrow so I could tell you all about the turkey dinner, but I'll probably be too lazy after that meal to do any writing.

We are going to have that turkey after all. It just came in and a more welcome sight I've never seen. We also had two fresh eggs per man for breakfast today and I don't know what to make of all this sudden luxury. Almost forgot- we had steak for dinner the other day too. This letter probably reads like a gourmet's dream, but when it's been so long since that kind of food has been served, I think it's worth writing about.

Went to the show last nite and saw Jack Benny in "George Washington Slept Here" and it wasn't bad at all. This letter makes this place sound like a vacation paradise, but you should see what goes on between these shows and these meals. Phooey on it! Well guys- I'll say goodbye again. Say "Hello" to everyone for me and write soon....

As ever,
Joe

November 29, 1943

Hello Gang,

Little did I dream when I sent that ring that it would cause all that furor. It's nothing to get excited over, but I'm glad you liked it so much. Haven't been able to do any good for Kay or the boys yet, but I haven't forgotten them.

The news is four days old now, but the event was such an occasion that I'll have to say a few words about our Thanksgiving feast. We had fresh turkey, fresh potatoes and pumpkin pie and all the usual trimmings with the exception of cranberries, which for some reason or other were omitted. It was a welcome change-getting away from dehydrated foods even for one meal. Now I'm wondering what Christmas will have to offer.

Had two letters from Brownie's spouse yesterday, but still no words from Brown.

Have heard that Gary Cooper and a small group of Hollywood actors are in the area and that we will get to see them. That won't be a bad event, tho I would rather see a boat heading for the States, but that will come someday. Well, I am about out of space again so I'll say goodbye until next time. Give my best to all and write soon.

As ever,
Joe

Timeline of the 158th Regimental Combat Team December 1943

December 12, 1943
The 2nd Battalion (Joe's group) is designated the reserve element for the upcoming invasion of New Britain Island.

December 15, 1943
U.S. troops land at Arawe, New Britain.

December 21, 1943
Reserves are called up.

December 25, 1943
Joe's unit, Company G of the 158th, is the first to be called up, and leaves Goodenough Island on a ferry boat to Finschhafen. They land there on December 26, 1943 and board three fast moving P.T. boats bound for Arawe, under the command of Lt. Orville Cochran.

December 10, 1943

Hello Gang,

I suppose I am due a scolding for this long delay since my last letter, but I really have been unavailable. I have had to neglect everyone this last week and I don't know how I'm going to get caught up.

We have had a trickle of Christmas mail these last two days and I drew a rather nice package of some much-needed articles from a gal I used to run around with when we were in Texas. I finally received the box of Pocket Readers that I ordered about five months ago so it does look like I'll do alright this year. It's the damndest thing - getting Christmas gifts with the temperature around 100 all the time. It don't seem natural.

Did I tell you we were paid a visit by some movie stars last week? Gary Cooper, Uma Mendel, and a chick by the name of Phyllis Brooks. The gals were the first white women we have seen in nine months and I should have gotten a bigger kick out of seeing them. I did, but the crowd was so big it took all the fun out of the thing. Had a letter from Brownie's Al last week, but I still haven't heard from him. Have you heard that Virginia had her appendix out? I'll have to say bye again. Am still well and hoping all of you are the same. Say "Hello" and write soon....

As ever,
Joe

Saturday, December 11 (the day before being called up to Arawe)
Hello Gang,

   You will have to forgive me again for not answering sooner. Your second letter arrived yesterday and it's all I can do to answer both of them at one time. I have a bit of discouraging news for you at this time. Maybe you won't think it's so bad, but I do. Censorship being what it is, I can't say too much about anything, but I can say that if you don't hear from me for the next month or two, don't think that I don't want to write or that I have gone off and forgotten all about you. It will just be that I'm going to be too busy to write.

   Finally found time to have the pictures taken and now it's just a question of waiting until they are finished. I don't think they will be ready in time to get to you in time for Christmas, but as soon as they are done, I will send them if possible. Speaking of Christmas and presents, if this letter gets to you in time to stop it, don't mail the present you have been talking about. I'll always be thankful for the thought, but don't send it.

   Had a letter from home the other day, telling me of all the snow you have been having. I sure would like to frolic around in some of the stuff just one time, even though I would no doubt freeze to death inside of ten minutes.

   I suppose that since John stopped over at the house, you have heard all about the latest escapade of Evelyn's. I meant to write you about it last letter, but it slipped my mind. Seems like she went off and got herself married to some jerk without waiting for the formality of a divorce. The handsome hero finally got wise to her and now is threatening her with bigamy charges. If you haven't heard the story, tell me next letter and I'll give you more of the details.

Your telling me of the laughs you got out of John's walking reminded me of how hard it was for me to get used to it when I first got in the army. It's a little tough at first, but it's good practice against the day when he may be called up for service. Walking isn't bad- just a matter of getting used to it.

Well gang, it's getting late and I had better start saying my goodbyes before the lights go out on me. Give my best regards to Grandma, the folks, Tony and Laura, Joy and Janet and everyone else. Think of me now and then and keep writing as often as you can, even though you probably won't hear from me for the next couple of months. So goodbye again until later and -

Love to all as ever,
Joe

Almost forgot. A Merry Christmas and Happy New Year to all. Joe

Timeline of the 158th Regimental Combat Team
January- February 1944

January 5, 1944
Company G of the 158th goes ashore at Arawe. They join the 112th Calvary from Texas, in need of combat support and relief. They are assigned a defense sector on the southern beaches of the peninsula. Company B is preparing to join them. By the end of the week, Company G successfully brings down a Japanese Zero equipped with a 50-caliber machine gun.

January 16, 1944
After several weeks of heavy fighting, the 158^{th,} along with the 112th Calvary and the First Marines Division 1st Tank Battalion launch a major offensive. This attack successfully breaks the Japanese defense at Cape Merkus, New Britain. Using light tanks from the 1st Marine Division, the 2nd Battalion attacks with Companies F and G together on the line. By late morning, G Company successfully overruns 20 Japanese pillboxes, thus reaching their objective. As the day progresses, reports indicate that the Japanese are beginning to withdraw. By the next day, they are completely defeated. The battle at Arawe is referred to as the "Baptism of Fire," as it is the first battle engagement for the Bushmasters. The Second Battalion of the 158th loses fifteen men and officers, and the Japanese have 192 casualties.

February 1944
The 2nd Battalion returns to Finschhafen to replace their losses from Arawe and to rejoin with the 1st and 3rd Battalions coming from Woodlark and Kiriwana, thus returning them to full strength. Company F moves to the Itni River and captures eleven Japanese landing barges and a gunboat. After three days of heavy fighting, the Japanese are defeated from Arawe to Gasmata.

February 20, 1944
New Britain is secure. Cape Gloucester has been taken back. Other major forces overcome the Japanese Air and Naval base in Rabaul, helping to cement victory in this campaign.

Following Arawe, the 158th Regimental Infantry Team earns the distinctive title change to the 158th Regimental Combat Team.

January 1, 1944

Hello Gang:

Well. How does the dawn of this New Year find you? With a slight case of hangover and a lot of resolutions to be broken? I imagine New Year's there was a dull affair this year. It already was the dullest and at the same time the most exciting one I've ever spent. I prefer the dull every time. Don't seem like it, but day before yesterday made two years out of the States for us. It's been a grand adventure and I wouldn't have missed a minute of it, but I'm ready to call it a day and come home for a while now. Who knows-maybe this year will be the lucky one for us. I hope so.

It's been a long time since I last wrote to you, but it was unavoidable, so I hope I'm forgiven. I was actually surprised to hear that John had met up with my ex and her sister. I can imagine why Violet wanted my address. Is Ev still married or has that crashed too? I imagine it has-she being what she is. I'm sure glad I got out of it with a whole skin.

I will have to say bye again. You may not hear from me as regularly as heretofore, because of a temporary shortage of V-mail paper, but I'll write as often as possible. Am still well and hoping this letter finds all of you the same. Say "Hello" to all for me and write when you can....

As always,
Joe

January 13, 1944

Hello Gang:

It looked for a while as tho I would never find the time to write you and I guess that you are thinking that I've forgotten you, but it's been the same old story- no time. It doesn't seem as tho anyone could ever get as busy as to not have the time to dash off a page of this V-mail and I don't think anyone is ever that occupied- it's just that at times writing letters is the last thing in the world you can get around to for various reasons. I don't make myself very clear, but someday I hope to explain. Until then, you will have to forgive these occasional lapses.

Glad to hear you had such a nice Christmas this year. I think I've already told you what sort of a day we had, so we'll say no more. We had a bit of a laugh the other day when one of the boys received a package that contained of all things- Christmas tree decorations- snow and tinsel and stuff like that there. We are still wondering if the sender was serious. I still haven't had all the packages that were sent, so must come to the conclusion that they met up with Davey Jones.

Things have been rather hectic for a while, but we are showing signs of coming back to normal- I guess your newspapers have been having a field day lately. One of the boys received a news clipping yesterday telling about some of the happenings and he laughed and laughed- why? I'll tell you some day.

Well guys-will say bye again. Found time to write to El
the other day - the first time I've written her in weeks,
but had to address to you as I lost hers.
Did you hear that regular mail sent by air gets here
faster than V-mail? I hope you can take the hint. Say
"Hello" to all and write often...

Love,
Joe

January 19, 1944 (post Arawe)

Hello Gang,

Your V-mail and Milly's letter both arrived together proving that the service is just as fast for one as for the other. I was glad to hear from you as I always am, but I don't feel like a traitor when I say that Milly's letter was very much enjoyed. There is something about this V stuff that seems to me to be rather cold and impersonal. It's so much better to get a regular letter, so again I say "Why don't you write your future letters in that manner."

You were more prompt in relaying the latest news than my father. It was a complete surprise- the news that the big fella is going to get married and settle down on the coast. He must have been plenty busy courting the gal, because I haven't heard from him in months. Haven't heard from Brownie yet, but as you know, I've long given up on the guy.

Your news about the Bears was very welcome indeed. I have heard a rumor that they had taken a beating from the Redskins again and the boys were sort of rubbing it in, but ever since your letter came they have been rather quiet.

Your remarks about seeing white gals soon again has me a bit puzzled. I hope I didn't give you the wrong impression in one of my letters, because so far as I know it will still be some time before those white gals appear on the scene again. We are hearing a lot about the bills that Congress is discussing in regards to bringing back those of us who have been overseas for a year or more, but there is not a thing definite.

Since we are now on our third year away from the States, I don't see how they can keep us much longer. Seems they should let us come home to show off all the damn ribbons we have earned and boost the morale up a little. And about keeping a close guard on me- if I can get to Chicago intact, I'll probably be okay. It's the first gal I see after getting off the boat that's got me worried. I'll probably tie up with her before I get my first Calvert and Coke.

Still haven't any news beyond what I gave you in my last letter- no shows, no women, no whiskey, no nothing, but the eternal tropical heat and equally eternal battle of the survival of the fittest.

I wonder if you've ever seen mention of my regiment in the paper back home? I suppose that since it is made up of boys from Arizona that they have heard of us out there, but what about the Chi papers. Well gang- I'll have to say goodbye again. I'm hoping Suzy got over her touch of flu and is well again. I'm still as well as could be expected and beginning to believe I'll make it. Give my best to all and write when you can find the time.

As Ever,
Joe

January 26, 1944

Hello Gang,

Received your two very nice letters and this one time I'm going to take advantage of you and answer both of them with this one. We went for a week without a mail call, and then came the great day and I suddenly found myself with no less than fourteen letters. It's going to take some writing to get them all answered - wouldn't be too tough if I had a table, but phooey on this foxhole.

Things are rather quiet again, in fact, they are almost too quiet. We are finding a little spare time now and then, but there is nothing to do with it. No shows, no news, no radio, no nothing. It's sure putting us behind the times again.

I wonder if you've read anything about us in the papers lately. We have heard that some nice things have been said about us, and naturally we are burning with curiosity. Let me know should you see an item.

I had a long letter from El and I was surprised, because she's usually so brief. Also heard from the big fella all the details of his marriage- he certainly didn't lose any time-only knowing the girl for two weeks. He is now living in Fresno, Cal and I'll have to stop in and pay my respects when I get back. Don't know if there's anything to it, but I've got high hopes of getting back soon now. Keep your fingers crossed for me.

Well gang- I'll say bye for now and will write again as soon as I get caught up. Give my best to everyone and let me hear from you soon....

As always,
Joe

February 4, 1944
Hello Gang,

  I can't remember ever having so much trouble trying to get caught up on my letter writing. We have been having a mail call every four days and generally there are from three to six letters. I just can't seem to catch up. Was just about to settle down and answer your letter of the 11ᵗʰ when I received the one of the 18ᵗʰ so here I am- way behind again.

  Things certainly did happen in the week between the two letters. We have heard a few words about the dog fighting of the pre- Pearl Harbor Fathers, but haven't paid much attention to it. As a rule, the boys don't care very much about who or what is being drafted. We have more fun discussing the great day when we are going to get home again.

  Haven't heard from Janet recently, so the news that Joy is 1-A was really a surprise. I never thought it would come to that. How are Joy and Al Nosek reacting to the idea? Janet told me some time ago that Joy was thinking of joining the Merchant Marine, so maybe he will like the idea of being a soldier.

  Nice to hear that Brownie received my letters. He hasn't taken the time or trouble to answer them yet, but I suppose since he mentioned them to you he will get around to it one of these days. I wish he would write, as a lot of the fellows that were in training camp with me are in the same theatre as he is, and possibly I could get in touch with them through him. Alberta has been writing on and off for some time and keeping me posted on his doings.

  That cottage on Little St. Germaine sounds like just the thing, but don't you think it's a bit too far from the city? You remember before the folks bought at Wandawega they were going to buy at Big Crooked Lake, then decided against it because of the distance. It's hell to have a nice place of your own and not be able to go there as much as you like because of travel time.

Am still wondering if you've seen mention of us in the papers. Be sure and send me any clippings you might notice, as I am still as curious as a cat.

Nothing new in the way of writable news. Everything about the same as last letter-just going along from day to day-and hoping and waiting for the great day. Everything goes well during the day but oh, those lonely nights.* Gives a guy plenty of time to think of his past, present, and future. Sure wish we had a movie to break the monotony of things but that's just an idle dream hereabouts.

Still haven't heard anything definite, but I can't shake the feeling that it won't be too much longer before I get back. Guess I won't have any trouble finding one of the surplus women - what's worrying me is that the States will probably run out of drinking whiskey before I can get my share.

Well guys, will say goodbye again- Give my best to all and write soon...

As Ever,
Joe

*Combat Operations mandated a strict policy of no movement during the night in the jungle. Staying in one's foxhole at night was the surest way to see the light of day.

February 10, 1944

Hello Gang,

These cockeyed mail calls we have been having lately sure have got me humping. Seems like every time I get caught up on my mail, we have a new call and then it's the same old story. Trying to find the time to answer anywhere from six to ten letters. Yesterday it was eight and today - the inevitable headache. Now don't get me wrong and stop writing - I always can find the time to write to you. I guess I just feel like groaning today.

Sorry to hear that the deal for the home in Arlington Heights fell thru. I was planning on visiting the folks there when I got back, but maybe they will work it out before then - I hope so.

What gives with the summer home you spoke of? Have you run into a stymee on that too!

I'm having a hell of a time getting this written. One of the boys is just outside trying to split some coconut logs so he can joist a roof on his foxhole. He's using a tent stake for a wedge and he keeps socking it and it always lands about fifteen feet away. The first sergeant and I are ribbing the hell out of him, because he comes from the lumber country around Eagle River, Wisconsin, and is supposed to know all about splitting rails. I guess he is nothing but a cheese maker after all.

Still haven't anything new on my favorite subject, except that it looks more promising every day. I'm still having a time convincing myself about "its" time. Well guys - will have to say bye again. Am still well and hoping this letter finds all of you the same. Give my best to everyone and write soon.

As ever, Joe

February 25, 1944 (Finschhafen)
Hi Gang,

Your letter came along yesterday and as far as I'm concerned, it saved the week. The mail has been acting up again- only one mail call in the last ten days and yours was the only letter I got. Serves one right for always complaining about not having the time to answer letters. Now I'm wishing I had a few to answer.

Last time I did have some mail I found a surprise package- a letter from my ex-sister-in law Violet. She told me John had given her my address and she really out did herself writing a nice letter. I won't go into the details, because I don't think you would be interested. The war and the army have certainly upset that family's way of life.

Things are getting better day by day. We now have a post exchange and believe it or not- I had a chocolate bar and a can of peanuts the other day. We were also paid a surprise visit by John Wayne last week. I don't know how we got this far away from civilization, but we did. Didn't have much to offer, but it helped to pass the time away. We have been promised movies in the very near future and that is something.

Still nothing definite about coming home, but I should have something on that soon too! Everything else is still normal- Plenty of heat and exercise not to mention corned willy.* Still feeling tip dash top except for a nagging pain in the back that refuses to go away.

Well kids- I'll have to run now. Will write again soon I promise. Say "Hello" to everyone for me and don't forget to write often.

As ever,
Joe

Corn Willy Hash

Made from the always plentiful supply of canned corned beef,

a.k.a. Willy, Sir William and [plain] Bill.   **Serves 4**

3 cups chopped cooked or frozen potatoes	1/4 cup butter
4 cups chopped cooked or canned corn beef	Fresh Ground Pepper

Combine potatoes and corned beef. Melt butter in a heavy skillet. Add 3/4 cup boiling water or hot broth left from cooking corned beef. Add potatoes and beef mixture. Season to taste with pepper. Cook over very low heat about 15 minutes or until a brown crust has formed on lower side of hash. Fold over and place on hot serving dish. Add poached eggs on top for the classic brunch dish.

From: The Early American Cookbook

Timeline of World War II in the South Pacific 1943

February 1-9, 1943
The U.S. has finally reached victory in Guadalcanal. This is an important victory, because it allows the U.S. a good location to begin penetrating Japanese holdings in the Pacific.

February 12, 1943
Japanese send more forces to New Guinea.

March 2-5, 1943
While in route to New Guinea, a Japanese convoy in the Bismarck Sea is bombarded by U.S. and Australian aircraft. All transports are sunk, as well as 4 destroyers. Roughly only 900 soldiers out of 4000 finish the journey to New Guinea.

April 7-13, 1943
Japanese launch air attacks in the Solomon Islands and New Guinea. Port Moresby, Milne Bay, and Guadalcanal are the targets of this mission. The offense is weak, perhaps indicating the Japanese have lost most of their well-trained pilots.

April 14, 1943
The plane carrying Isoroku Yamamoto, Commander of Japan's Navy, is shot down by two U.S. bomber planes. The attack is pre-planned and ordered by the Secretary of the Navy and President Roosevelt.

June 20, 1943
U.S. Sixth Army establishes headquarters at Milne Bay.

August 17, 1943
U.S. aircraft attack the Japanese 4th Army Air Base at Wewak on the northern coast of New Guinea. Seventy five percent of Japanese aircraft is destroyed, leaving 38 planes.

September 4, 1943
The Australian 9th Division lands at Lae in the Huon Gulf, New Guinea.

September 12, 1943
The Allies take Salamaua back in the Huon Gulf in New Guinea.

September 16, 1943
Lae is taken back from Japan. The victories (Lae and Salamaua) give the Allies a vital port and airfield in New Guinea.

October 2, 1943
Australian forces take back Finschhafen. The coastline of the Huon Peninsula in New Guinea is now secure.

October 12, 1943
Rabaul, New Britain is attacked by air. The Allies drop over 20,000 tons of bombs.

October 21, 1943
The Japanese government grants the Philippines independent status, which carries no value.

December 15, 1943
U.S. army troops land on the Arawe Peninsula in southern New Britain.

December 29, 1943
The airfield at Cape Gloucester is seized by the Allies. This will provide vital safe airspace between New Guinea and New Britain.

December 31, 1943
Bougainville in the Solomon Islands has a fully operational U.S. Navy Base with 3 airstrips.

Part V
Dutch New Guinea
1944

"The guy that said that there are no atheists in a foxhole knew what he was talking about."

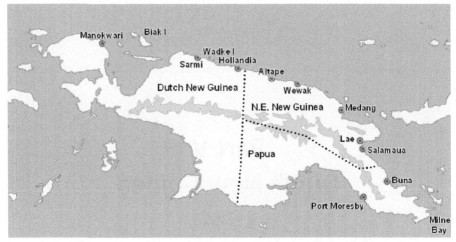

Map Courtesy of Arizona State University

Early in 1944, the Allies ramped up their takeback of New Guinea. The success of Operation Cartwheel brought the Solomon Islands into the hands of the Americans, and successfully isolated the Japanese stronghold, Rabaul, located on New Britain Island. This made way for Phase 4 in the New Guinea Campaign, which involved troops leapfrogging up the rugged Japanese-occupied northern coast of Dutch New Guinea. (Western New Guinea) The coast was 1200 miles long with Japanese bases strategically located throughout. The terrain was laden with mangrove swamps, often crocodile infested, with high cliffs that required scaling by rope. Success in this phase would finally clear the way for MacArthur's ultimate destination: The Philippines.

Allied forces recaptured Hollandia by surprise in April 1944. The Japanese were prepared for an attack on Wewak, a fortified base with several airfields. Instead, MacArthur decided to go up the coastline and take Hollandia. The capture of Hollandia and nearby Aitape separated the Japanese Army on the north coast into two separate parts. This opened the door to Wakde-Sarmi, where other Japanese air bases were located.

The Bushmasters left Finschhafen and headed to Toem, where they became part of the Tornado Task Force. Toem is located on the mainland of New Guinea, across from Wakde Island. The 163rd RCT, also part of Tornado Task Force, was able to capture Wakde Island in three days, at the cost of 40 American lives versus 800 Japanese lives. The capture of Wakde Island secured one air base, however, this would be futile without also controlling the bases at Maffin and Sawar near Sarmi on the mainland.

In order to reach these targets, the Bushmasters had to cross two rivers and a range of hills, all within Japanese territory. U.S. Intelligence estimated there were about 6,500 Japanese in the Sarmi area, but only 4,000 of them were combat soldiers. The 163rd RCT and the 158th RCT, together totaled 10,000 men. In actuality, the Japanese manpower far exceeded the Intelligence estimates. The newly formed Yuki group, which included the Japanese 36th Tiger Division was comprised of fierce soldiers with great fighting experience from previous takeovers in China and Malaya. Some soldiers in this group came from the northern island of Hokkaido and were as tall as 6 feet, which was an unusual sight for the American soldiers, who were accustomed to a shorter enemy.

The 158th began crossing the Tor River only to be stopped by the Japanese. The Japanese continued their offense by launching Bonzai attacks. Along with the 3rd Battalion of the 224th Infantry, the 158th responded with a vicious offense and were able to continue their advance to the airstrip.

The advance took them through a coast of coral ridgeline and a rain forest that was dominated by a large tree. Army Intelligence didn't think it would be too treacherous, as all maps indicated there was a single tree, so they assumed there was no jungle. It turned out to be a large rain forest dominated by one mangrove tree with large thick heavy roots above the ground. Later, it was jokingly referred to as Lone Tree Hill. Despite a strong enemy and treacherous conditions, the Bushmasters were ordered to take Lone Tree Hill. Their advance slowed down as they worked their way through the thickness.

MacArthur grew impatient with the slow advancement. He became more dissatisfied after he sent General Patrick, Commander of the Tornado Task Force, to visit Colonel Prugh Herndon, Commander of the 158th, in the field. Herndon was a leader with strong loyalty to his men. He surmised that the Japs were stronger than anticipated, well-dug in and prepared to ambush the Bushmasters. Herndon requested General Patrick's permission to retreat, and it was granted. Herndon's action likely saved many of his Bushmasters, but ultimately cost him his command. MacArthur immediately replaced Herndon with Colonel Earl "Bulldog" Sandlin. The Bushmasters literally wept as they said goodbye to their beloved leader. History has shown that Herndon's decision to retreat was the right call.

The Bushmasters carried on with Tornado Task Force and were able to continue their advance. On one night alone, the 2nd Battalion fought off eight different Japanese attacks. Tokyo Rose* referred to the Bushmasters as the "Butchers of the Pacific." After four long weeks of battle and treacherous movement, the Bushmasters were relieved by the 6th Army Division. This spoke well for them, as they were relieved by an entire division. It took another six weeks for the 6th Army to overtake Lone Tree Hill and capture the airfield at Sarmi. This airfield turned out to be one of the largest Japanese bases in the South Pacific. Control of the airfield was vital for further operations on Biak, Noemfoor, and Voglekop

Peninsula, located on the northwestern tip of New Guinea. Without Sarmi, the Japanese offensive was no longer effective in New Guinea.

Noemfoor was the final stop for the Bushmasters on their journey through New Guinea. Noemfoor is an island located between the island of Biak and the Vogelkop Peninsula, located on the tip of Dutch New Guinea. The Japanese were using the island as a staging area for troops moving into Biak. Just four days after being relieved at Wakde-Sarmi, the Bushmasters were included in the plans for Operation Noemfoor, whose main objective was to extend air operations on the northern coast of New Guinea.

Compared to their last engagement, Noemfoor was a walk in the park. This was largely due to the fact that the landscape was coral. This meant that there was little brush, so one of their enemies was eliminated: the jungle.

On July 1, 1944, Tokyo Rose stated, "The Bushmasters are about to land at Noemfoor where they will find a wall of steel." True to form, this propaganda couldn't have been further from the truth. With air support from the U.S. 5th Air Force and the Royal Australian Air Force, the Bushmasters, along with the 147th Field Artillery arrived on the beaches at Noemfoor on July 2, 1944. The objective was to overtake Kamari airstrip and then reconstruct it to accommodate B-29 Bombers. This goal was met quickly, and fifteen days after it was overtaken, it was ready for General MacArthur to land there. By August 31, 1944, the Bushmasters were able to report that Operation Noemfoor was complete. They remained on the island for four more months, presumably enjoying some quiet time.

The fifth and final phase of the New Guinea Operation involved "mopping up" the remaining Japanese troops. By the time this phase began, the Bushmasters were well on their way to their final adventure of fulfilling MacArthur's "I shall return" promise.

*Tokyo Rose was the name given to broadcaster Iva Toguri by American soldiers. She was a Japanese American living in Japan at the outbreak of World War II. The Japanese insisted she renounce her American citizenship, but she refused. After repeated harassments from military police, she moved to Tokyo and took a job as a typist at Radio Tokyo, where she eventually joined Major Charles Cousens, a captured Australian military officer, who was being forced to broadcast propaganda on the show "The Zero Hour." Together, they covertly satirized the Japanese messages. Ironically, she was convicted of treason by a U.S. court in 1949. In 1977, she was pardoned by President Gerald Ford.

Timeline of the 158th Regimental Combat Team
March-May 1944

March-May 1944

It is presumed the Bushmasters are in the area around Finschhafen and will leave for Toem in May 1944, where their next battle will take place.

March 5, 1944

Hello Gang,

Have been slowly but surely going gray these past four days. Trying to find the time to answer your letter of the 2nd of February and this morning there was another. Don't misunderstand that remark and stop writing now; it wasn't meant that way. It's just that it bothers me to have letters around to be answered and no time. I won't take advantage of you and answer both of yours with just this page of V-mail, but will write again in a day or two.

Had a letter from Milly too with picture enclosed. It did more than anything else could have done to make me realize how much things really have changed since the last time I was home. I'm still finding it hard to believe that she has changed so. I showed it to several of the boys (showing the pictures you get from home is a ritual around here) and I wouldn't want to tell her the many compliments I heard. It would give her a swelled head.

Well guys- tomorrow's the big day- the debut of our movie. Don't know yet what's to be shown but after two months without I'm not worried- I could enjoy "Buck Jones."

We had some new boys sent to the company a few days ago and one of them comes from Arlington Heights. He has only been away from Chicago for five months now and you can bet that I am pumping him dry of information every time I can corner him. I don't know whether to believe all of the things he has been telling me tho. He makes Chi sound like someplace I've never been to. Is it as bad as all that? What about that ten women for every 4-F? What pluckins!

170

Well, I see I'm down to the bottom again so will say "Give my best to everyone" and I will write in a few days. Until then…..

As always,
Joe

Still nothing new on coming home, but I'm still keeping my dainty fingers crossed.

March 13, 1944

Hi Gang,

Well- Here I am with that promised letter, but it still don't answer the problem. I had another from you yesterday and that still leaves me one down. One of these fine days I will get caught up and the good Lord willing- I intend to stay caught up.

I've certainly done a lot of corresponding with the Hudec and Faber families recently. Wrote to Grandma a short time ago - wrote two letters to you, one to Lou's mother and Lady Eleanore and still have one from Milly that I hope to answer today. Gosh- I hope you don't pass them around because for the best part of them they are just repeats and you will find out what a fraud I am. No kidding tho - you can't appreciate what a job it is writing letters under censorship regulations until you have tried it. The toughest job I ever tackled. Shouldn't complain tho, think of the bull sessions when I get back.

You have made at least two references in your recent letters about the meetings of "The Secret Pal Club". Just what in the hell is the object of an outfit with a name like that? Is it a false front-an excuse to get together and guzzle beer or are you in your second childhood? Who are the members, the president? I would like to wager a few bucks that John is treasurer. Give out some of the details, huh?

Well-after all this time we are once again seeing movies. Have had two in the last week and it looks like they are here to stay. Saw "Legs" Grable in "Coney Island" first, and last night they showed Humphrey Bogart in "Sahara." I like the first one very much, but didn't think too much of "Sahara." I see enough soldiers and army life seven days a week to satisfy me.

172

I hear the next picture will be "*Girl Crazy*" and since all of us are just that-it should make a big hit.

Lou's mother enclosed a clipping in her letter about the soldiers returning from overseas business and as good as the news was- it was just a little disappointing. For some unknown reason (we never have a reason) we had ourselves believing that we would get a sixty-day furlough when we got back, and the news that they were only giving the boys twenty-one days was sort of a let-down. Imagine worrying about how much of a furlough I will get when there is still the problem of getting back to be worked out. There is still nothing new on that subject, but I refuse to lose faith yet.

I was very much intrigued by Lou's description of the new hook she has developed in her bowling. I sure would like to see that southpaw slant-and with speed too. My-my! How things have changed.

Well guys-I'll have to close for now. I want to write to Milly before it gets too late and thank her for the picture. (Did you know she sent me a picture? A damned nice one too.)

Say "Hello" to all for me. Am still well and hoping this letter finds all of you the same.

As always,
Joe

March 20, 1944

Hello Gang,

This letter will of necessity have to be a short one, because two sheets of this paper is all I have for the time being. Got a few sheets of V-mail, but I won't use them until it becomes absolutely necessary.

I'm glad you are intending to send some news clippings. Maybe I can catch up on things a bit. It's funny how you can be smack in the middle of things and yet know so little of what's happening.

Sorry- but I can't enlighten you as to our whereabouts. We're not allowed to say, but your guesses are way off the track. I'm surprised that you haven't seen something in the papers. They made quite a splash about us not long ago.

Had a letter from Brownie's Alberta the other day, and she said something about seeing you just before the holidays. And speaking of bowling- which I wasn't, she tells me of the 185 game she bowled and of numerous 170 games. Makes them sound like an everyday occurrence, which is putting it on a bit thick.

Too bad Suzy hasn't brought her game that high. What a match game they could bowl. Just imagine both of them giving their all and winding up with the number 200- between the two of them.

Nothing of importance since my last letter. Everything is still going along from day to day. Saw another show the other night Carey Grant in "Mr. Lucky." We don't have too many, but those we do are always good.

I don't want to make you poor rationed civilians envious, but I can't resist telling you of the steak we have been having. Well- it was only two meals, but the first fresh meat since how have you been. Even fresh potatoes and butter. If this keeps up (which it probably won't) they will have me wanting to stay here.

Still haven't heard any more about coming home- It's still in the probable stage, but the time it will take to get back is still vague.

Well guys- Will have to close for now. Give my best to everyone and write soon....

As always,
Joe

March 25, 1944

Hello Gang,

I thought I had managed to put this business of writing letters on V-mail behind me for life, but there is a temporary shortage of stamps hereabouts and rather than put off writing for two or three days, I decided to go against my principles just this once. We are having one of our rare rainy days today, and as a result, things are rather quiet for a change.

We had our first payday in months the other day and for the 2nd time in my army career I was red-lined. I signed the payroll with this green ink and it seems the Finance Officer frowns on such goings on. Not getting paid didn't prevent me from taking the beating of my life in a poker game. They tore my hide off and hung it on the back fence to dry to the tune of sixty-five pounds. That's enough to point a bed path three miles wide all the way from Frisco to this. This is probably the only place in the world where a guy could lose that kind of dough and not feel bad about it. There's nothing else to do with it so what the hell...

Things have been very quiet since my last letter - even a bit dull. We are seeing some good pictures, the food is improving, we have had steak, fresh butter and potatoes several times since I last wrote - so the only thing left to gripe about is when are we coming home. Haven't heard anything more about it, but it still looks very promising.

Well guys - I'll say bye for a few days. Will write again when stamps are available and until then... Give my best to everyone and write soon.

As always,
Joe

March 29, 1944
Somewhere in the Southwest Pacific
Hello Gang,
   Maybe the heading of this letter will explain why I
stopped heading my letters. It's the only one we are
allowed to use and it's so vague that there didn't
seem any point in using it. I was surprised to hear
that you don't know where we are. Censorship forbids
our saying, but it's public news at home having been
in all the papers recently. I have received some
clippings telling me where I'm at and what I'm doing
and I can't say a word about it. Confusing as hell,
but that's the Army every time. Knowing what a nose
for news John has, I would bet money that he had
heard all about it. He must be slipping in his old age.
Anyway-if you really want to know, call Virginia.
   As for your asking questions in your letters - I know
of no reason why you shouldn't. Your letters are never
censored and even if they were, there's no harm in
asking. I won't promise to answer them, but I'll do the
best I can -as far as censorship regulations permit.
Shouldn't be too much longer before I can give you
some of the answers in person. The odds are getting
shorter every day, but of course you can never tell -
things change so often.
   If this place gets much nicer it's going to be hard to
leave it. They are certainly doing their best to make
up for the time we had to do without things. We see a
show every night (and all the best pictures too). The
food is so much better; there is no comparison. We
have been getting fresh meat on the average of one
meal a day and you can't appreciate what that
means until you have tried living on c-rations and
corn willy for a couple of months. There is a rumor

177

going around that there are oysters to be found in the bay and some of us are going down to try our luck one of these days.

To top it all off- the weather has been just about perfect. Not too hot and not too wet. What more can a guy ask. Well, maybe Wine, Women, and Song, but then you can't have everything.

Don't believe I told you that we had a payday- the first in months not long ago. Didn't do me much good, because I signed the payroll with this green ink and as a result I was red-lined. Borrowed enough to get in a few poker games and I couldn't have more money even if I had been paid. This letter doesn't sound right-nothing to complain about.

Well guys- I'll have to cut this short- it's just about time to eat. Say "Hello" to everyone for me and I'll be waiting to hear from you soon....

As always,
Joe

April 6, 1944

Hello Gang,

Your letter with news clipping enclosed arrived the other day and I enjoyed both very much. Can't tell you I liked the booklets you spoke of, because they are still among the missing. Should be here most any day now tho.

Had a letter from Joy and Janet along with yours and it does look as tho Joy will be in uniform - probably he is already. Damn -there are some things I just can't understand. Taking married men without children is one thing, but breaking up families is another. We have a fellow in the company who left his wife and two kids (I should say he was taken) almost three and a half years ago. He hasn't seen them in twenty-eight months and I think that's piling it on just a little bit thick. Course - the way this war is moving these days, it will probably be over soon and it's not likely Joy will be away too long, but it's still a rough deal. Haven't heard from Eleanore in some time now and I'm wondering if she is forgetting me. Ask her how come.

I couldn't keep up with your remark about Frank working on his old new Ford. Sounds like another car. Is it an old gas saving jalopy to be used for going to work or is the motor to be used on the boat? Tell me about it next letter, huh.

This sweating out that boat ride back to the States is about to get me down. Out of the clear blue sky they have started the furloughs to Australia again. It doesn't change the plans for coming back to the States - just a sort of bonus for services rendered I guess. Since I am still quite a way down on the furlough list I doubt whether it will have any effect on me and I

179

don't really mind. A trip to Australia would probably cost two or three hundred bucks and that dough would come in handy when I get back. Will keep you posted on things as they develop.

Had a letter from the big fellow the other day and from the sound of it he is really happy in the service. Says he is marked in tenor zone duty which means he will never leave the States. He's happily married, lives off the post, has a car and gets plenty of time for fishing. Sounds like a position to me. I could go for some of that life myself - but without the frau.

Well guys- will say bye again. One of the boys just called and reminded me it's time to go fishing. John and Frank would certainly like to get in on some of that I know. Don't know the names of some of these babies we catch, but they are at least four-foot long and some fun. Will write again soon and until then- say "Hello" to all for me and keep your fingers crossed against a F.U.B.A.R...

As always,
Joe

April 11, 1944

Hi Gang,

Here I am again- and with V-mail. Am temporarily out of stationery and as much as I hate this stuff it's better than nothing. I'm up to my neck in letters again and don't know which to answer first- after this one. Had a letter from Janet telling me all about Joy's induction. Heard too from Alberta. First time in ages. Also, the long-expected letter from El. She is the optimist. Said she didn't write, because of the fear that I would be on my way home before the letter got to me. If that's not optimism, I'll put in with you.

Observed Easter yesterday in the usual manner. No eggs, no bunny, no nothin'. Just another day.

Have I told you that they have started giving furlough to Australia again? Looks like I may get to spend a week there before coming back if I decide to go. I think I'll take a pass though.

Have all but made up my mind to buy a car when I get back. What kind of a jalopy can you get for about seven hundred? I wish Frank or John would pass along a little information on the subject.

Well gang - this is all too brief, but I'll make up for it in a day or two. Say "Hello" to all and be good......

As ever,
Joe

The cheese-maker I referred to is one of the boys who comes from Wisconsin. What did you think?
Aside to Suzy- Why don't you give me the scores of your bad games as well as the good?

April 18, 1944

Hi Gang,

Your letter of the 27th of March arrived yesterday and also the booklet on Chicago's nite life. Seemed almost like old times -reading about the joints and all. I noticed so many new names - places I have never heard of but the address seemed familiar. Must be the old joints with new names, couldn't be so many new places. It's going to be fun rediscovering all the old places again.

We haven't been having any mail to speak of these last two weeks, in fact, I've had only two letters in that time. Don't know what the causes are, but we should have an avalanche of letters one of these days soon. Every so often the mail service goes JANFU on us.

Well guys- it looks now as tho I will get to see Australia once again before I see Chicago. The furloughs are moving along and it won't be too long now before my turn comes. I was seriously thinking of turning mine down, because I felt I didn't want to spend a lot of money just before coming home, but I just can't resist seeing civilization again after fourteen months in the jungle. Besides, it looks now as tho it will be almost Christmas before I get back, and life in these parts is too uncertain to pass up a little pleasure when you can get it.

Really haven't had anything to complain about these days tho. We're living the life of Riley. Nothing to do but fish, swim and play cards. Had a payday last week and it seems I've been playing about eight hours a day ever since. They brought the movie projector out last Friday and showed us a double feature. I guess we will have at least two pictures a week from now on.

The food is still improving too, even as I sit here writing, my stomach is digesting two very lovely fresh eggs I had for breakfast this morning.

Gosh, there certainly is a shortage of news around here. Absolutely nothing doing at all. The weather has been perfect except for an occasional shower, but I don't suppose you are interested in this summer weather of ours, now that you are having some of your own. Has the baseball season gotten underway yet? How do the Cubs and Sox figure to finish this year?

Well guys - that covers about everything for now. Should have a letter from you very soon now and will write again then. Say "Hello" to all for me, huh.

As always,
Joe

May 6, 1944

Hi Gang,

Have been intending to get this letter off for almost a week now, but this the first opportunity I've had. Your letter of the sixth of April arrived yesterday, so I'll answer it while I'm at it.

Well guys, they have finally eased up on the censorship regulations, and I can now put an end to the guessing games you have been indulging in and straighten you out a little as to where we have been and what we have been up to. I was surprised to hear that you were in the dark as to my whereabouts. All the papers carried the story and I know that John follows all of the news closely. Looks like the old master is losing his grip at last, but that's getting away from the subject.

We were in New Britain. I can't tell you where or how long we were there, but I think I can say that we were one of the first to set foot on the place.* Now that you know where I was, you can probably fill in the details from the news accounts. Believe me, it was hell on earth for a while, and even now when it's all over and done with, I still pinch myself once in a while to prove to myself that I'm still among the living. Many were the times when I thought that my number was up.

You no doubt remember some of those foolish arguments we used to have on the subject of religion. Well, it will probably be some source of satisfaction to Suzy and Eleanore to hear me admit that I think they were completely right. I think John would feel the same way as I do if he had ever had to go through that hell. Tojo's air force certainly made a preacher out of me. The guy that said, "There are no atheists in a foxhole" knew what he was talking about.

You probably know how it all ended, so I won't say anymore except that we kicked the living _____ out of them. Made those Nips wish they had never left Tokyo. Course, we left some boys behind when we came away, fellows that any man would be proud to call friend, but that's all part of this rotten business.

We are now back in New Guinea (and by the way, don't overlook the new address) where life has once again taken some semblance of normal. As I sit here writing, some of the boys are buzzing around on the roof of the tent putting in the wiring that should give us electric lights within the next few days. That's the first time in fourteen months anything like that has happened to us and I don't quite know what to make of it. Must be a catch in it somewhere.

As I told you last letter, they are giving furloughs to Australia again and it shouldn't be too much longer before it becomes my turn. As for getting back to the States, you can uncross your fingers, because the way things are going now it will still be some time before I get there.

Maybe I'm being too impatient, but it seems to me that it's moving too slow to do most of us any good. Looked for a while like I might make it for my birthday, but right now I would settle for the first of next year and consider myself lucky. Oh well, maybe things will speed up. I'll keep you posted.

Have you seen Claudette Colbert in "No Time for Love?" I saw it the other night and enjoyed it very much. Also saw "Thousands Cheer" and it was tops.

Haven't had the dozen steaks yet, but at the rate they are coming in, it won't be long now. I'll think of you poor rationed civilians every time I eat one.

Haven't heard from Janet in some time now, but she would hardly have the time for letters with Joy so close to leaving. Have John and Frank ever heard any more on their reclassification? From what little I have been able to read on the subject, it looks to me like they won't be satisfied until they get every man who is able to walk into uniform.

Haven't been able to get much news on the doings of the Cubs and Sox. I did hear that the Cubs got off to a good start, but I haven't been able to verify it. Could you send me the standings from time to time?

Well guys, will have to close for now. The boys on the roof are having their troubles, so I had better get out and give them a hand. Say "Hello" to everyone for me and write soon.

As Always,
Joe

*This letter is five months post Arawe, the battle he is referring to in this letter, which was the Bushmasters first battle. Joe's unit, Company G, was the first to be called up for the invasion of New Britain.

Timeline of the 158th Regimental Combat Team
May - June 1944

May 17, 1944

The 158th RCT lands at Toem in an attempt to divert Japanese soldiers fighting at Sarmi.

May 17-June 12, 1944

The Bushmasters battle with the Japanese 6th Army Tiger Division.

May 23, 1944

The 158th crosses the Tor River in order to advance on Maffin Airstrip. They are stopped by the Japanese. The 1st Battalion sees action as they relieve the 163rd RCT. The 3rd Battalion meets fierce opposition.

May 25, 1944

Bushmasters resume their advance to Maffin Airstrip on a coral ridge line with towering trees. (Lone Tree Hill) They are met with heavy resistance. Five days and nights of heavy fighting ensue.

May 27, 1944

By days end, almost 300 Bushmasters are either killed, wounded, or overtaken by exhaustion.

May 28, 1944

Bushmasters make it to the top of Lone Tree Hill only to find fortified Japanese territory below. Low on supplies and ammunition, they are forced to retreat. Colonel Prugh Herndon gets permission to retreat, but this will cost him his command, as MacArthur felt it showed weakness on his part.

May 29, 1944

Colonel Sandlin assumes command of the 158th RCT. Heavy fighting is resumed. The 3rd Battalion destroys a reinforced Battalion of the Japanese Tiger Division.

Tokyo Rose refers to the Bushmasters as the "Butchers of the Pacific."

June 5, 1944

The 158th continues their advance, engaging in fighting along the way.

June 11, 1944

The 158th is relieved by the entire 6th Army Division.

June 1, 1944

Hello Gang,

 You will have to overlook the V-mail and t⌐
this time. I haven't any other stationery abo⌐
for the writing, I'm surprised I can write at all. Your
letter arrived the other day and I can honestly say I
was never happier to hear from you. When I tell you of
the conditions under which I received it you will
understand why it meant so much to me.

 Haven't had my clothes off or even washed myself for
seven days now, and the only sleep I've had in that
time has been a catnap whenever and wherever
possible and believe me, I feel like I'm about ready to
give up any time now. Oddly, last letter I told you we
were back from New Britain and everything was jake.
What a laugh!

 Had a letter from El along with yours but don't
know if I will have the time or energy to write to her.

 Notice the new address. Seems like every letter I
write these days has a new A.P.O. It must be some job
for you keeping up with me.

 Well gang. That's all I have for now - will write
again as soon as possible. If you don't hear from me
for some time, get in touch with the folks. They will be
notified if anything happens to me. Give my love and
regards to everyone and... I'll be waiting to hear from
you.

                                            As always,
                                            Joe

The coming home business doesn't look as hot, but
what the hell, there's always next year.

                                            Joe

                        189

June 6, 1944
Hello Gang,

Had your swell letter yesterday and it certainly was good hearing from you again so soon. Never again will I complain about the army postal service. When and if I get back, you won't believe me when I tell you of the conditions under which the letters were delivered to us. No one was even expecting mail, so you can imagine how glad we were to hear from you.

Finally had that bath and change of clothes, but it took twelve days in coming. Talk about earning that trip back to the States - we are certainly doing it the hard way.

Had a letter from home along with yours, but they said nothing about Ginny going to California on her vacation. From all I've heard, she's doing pretty well by herself, so no doubt she can afford it. Also had a letter from Joy and Janet with the good news about Joy's army deferral at the last moment. I'll bet they were mighty glad to get that news.

I've got some Jap invasion money of a new kind for you, but I can't manage for an envelope so you will have to wait until next letter.

Will have to say bye until later. Am still as well as could be expected and hoping for the best. Haven't heard any news of any kind for two weeks now, but just heard a rumor that we have finally captured Rome. I wonder if you've been reading about us in the papers. Well give my best to everyone and write soon...

As ever,
Joe

Timeline of the 158th Regimental Combat Team
June – August 1944

June 16, 1944
Operation Noemfoor is being planned.

June 23, 1944
Noemfoor is surrounded by coral reefs, making a beach landing almost impossible. Alamo Scouts* from Company G go on a reconnaissance mission to determine the lay of the land.

July 1, 1944
Tokyo Rose states, "The Bushmasters are about to land at Noemfoor where they will find a wall of steel."

July 2, 1944
The Bushmasters land at Noemfoor with little Japanese resistance. The 1st Battalion crosses the Kamari River and meets enemy resistance. The 158th overruns and takes Kamari Airfield from the Japanese. It is then reconstructed to handle larger planes. Fifteen days later, General MacArthur lands there in a B-29 Bomber.

July 4, 1944
The 158th forges on to take Komasoren Airfield. The 3rd Battalion advances, where they meet light opposition and are able to secure the airstrip.

July 6, 1944
The 2nd Battalion lands on Roemboi Bay with the mission of seizing Namber Airfield. They meet little opposition and are able to secure the airstrip the same morning.

August 31, 1944
Bushmasters can report that The Operation Noemfoor is complete with mission accomplished.

*The Alamo Scouts were a top-secret reconnaissance and raider unit that operated in the Pacific during World War II. They are recognized by the army as a forerunner of the modern Special Forces. Many members of this elite group were Native Americans.

June 17, 1944
Dutch New Guinea (one week after being relieved by an entire army division)

Hello Gang,
I guess I've got all kinds of hell coming to me this time, but honestly, this is the first opportunity I've had for writing a letter in the last three weeks.

As you have probably noticed from the heading of this letter- we are now in Dutch New Guinea. I was surprised when told it was permissible to say something about it. Usually it takes just a little longer for them to lift the censorship lid. You have no doubt read all about it in the papers - it must have made a swell story.

Have had no less than five letters from you in the past ten days - the mail has really been getting to us in jig time lately. Troops in combat always get an A-1 priority on the delivery of mail. Good for the old morale I suppose.

I hope never to have to spend as hectic a three weeks as these last three have been -it was really rough. For example, I had two baths and changes of clothes in that time, so you can draw your own conclusions. Had my first night's sleep above the ground the other night and it was so damned unusual that I barely slept a wink. I've still got to get over that ground hog complex, I guess.

The outfit that relieved us was coming thru the other day, and I met a fellow who came into the army with me. The first time in three years I've met one of the boys who came in with me. The circumstances under which we met were such that we barely had time to say more than "Hello", but one of these days when things settle

193

down I'll look him up and have an old-fashioned bull-session.

I'm reading all of your letters and will try to give you the answers to all of your questions. First, all the pictures you sent are present and accounted for. The last two and a half years haven't brought about any changes in any of you. I wonder if I am withstanding the ravages of time as well. Did I ever mention that I'm down to 160 soaking wet? Doesn't seem to have hurt me either.

Just read another one of your epistles and I am chuckling - so you know that F.U.B.A.R. has something to do with a furlough, but you're not quite sure exactly what it means. Well, so far as I know, it has never had a thing to do with furloughs. It's an expression we have and the letters in the word represent words which go something like this: F is for fouled (we of course have several variations of fouled) U is for up, B is for beyond, A is for all and R is for recognition. Thus, when you say FUBAR you mean Fouled Up Beyond All Recognition. Get it!

(rest of letter is missing)

July 22, 1944

Hi Gang,

In spite of your admonition not to apologize for not writing more regularly, I have a guilty feeling and that's for sure. It doesn't seem possible that it's been a month since the last time I wrote to you, but it must be, because the calendar doesn't lie. I have been receiving your letters regularly and they have been a godsend to my weary morale.

You can imagine how very active we have been when I say that no one has had time for writing letters. They haven't lifted the censorship lid as yet, so I can't give you any of the details now, but maybe next letter we will be able to go into a few details. Possibly you have been reading of the doings of the Bushmasters in the papers and will know all about it.

Do you still save all of my letters? I suppose I should keep a diary of my travels, but since I don't, my letters to you will make the best index I can think of. So many things have happened to me since I came in to the army that I've all but forgotten most of them.

I have been out of action these past three days with a banged-up elbow. Got in the way of a knife* and wound up with a deep cut. The blade nicked the bone and the damned arm got stiff on me with the result that I couldn't do much good. The good Doc marked me light duty and that's what I've been doing - but light.

As is the custom thru these little maneuvers of ours, we have been subsisting mostly on a diet of dear old K-C rations for some time now, and although it looks like we will be going back to hot meals soon, the time is not yet.

195

Have also been getting along without our usual entertainment, which is to say - without shows. Our next movie is still uncertain, so I won't even say it will be soon.

I suppose that you deduced from my lack of letters that I am either in Australia on furlough or on my way back to the States. Well - I wish it were so, but nothing could be further from the truth. Fact is - the furlough seems to be "just one of those things that they used to give" and the going home policy has all but stopped, although it is understandable in view of what's been happening. There should be some really good news soon. We all hope so. Now, more than ever do I want to get back. I'm worried that my chest won't be big enough to wear all the battle stars and campaign ribbons we have earned and I would like to get away before I run out of chest space. All of which is another way of saying that I've had my share of the fighting and would like to settle down with carpet slippers for a while.

Had your (or rather John's) letter along with the horse races and enjoyed both of them very much. I turned up half-dozen of them to stimulate a little interest and next payday (whenever that may be. We haven't been paid for two months!) I expect to reap a fair profit. While on the subject of sports - the boys might be interested that I bet fifty skins at 3 to 1 that the Sox would win the pennant this year. Last time I heard (about three weeks) they were in second place and going strong.

We had some rookies come in as replacements recently and one of them had served as an MP on Howard Street before coming down here, so I'm all caught up on the doings at the Village Inn.

Well guys, I could go on and on, but a three-week pile of mail tells me to try and answer a few more. Will write again soon I promise and until then - say "Hello" to all and I'll be waiting to hear from you.

As always,
Joe

*I can't help but wonder if this knife wound was a result of hand to hand combat with a Japanese soldier. I remember a scar above my dad's left elbow and he always cradled that elbow. I never knew what caused it.
Mary Jo

August 3, 1944

Dearest John and Lou,

Well, catching up on all of my letter writing was quite a job, but I finally managed. Only thing is, while in the process of catching up, I have been getting letter after letter, not the least of which were three from you, so the net result is that I'm right back where I started. All of which is my way of saying that I'm going to answer all three of your letters with this one. I hope you won't mind; there really isn't enough I can say to fill three letters anyway.

Believe I told you last letter that I had a letter from Milly. Well. I didn't get around to answering her for some time and the other day I had another from her in which she mentioned writing earlier and expressing the opinion that the letter had probably been lost enroute. That is, the first letter. I've already written her and explained the long delay and I hope she will understand.

I still haven't made up my mind whether you were kidding when you asked if we have any crap games. What would the army be without dice and poker? We have the roughest games around the company that I ever hope to sit in. Most all of them are no limit, and with a little luck it's not at all unusual for a guy to win a thousand dollars in one evening's play. Best I ever did in one night was four hundred plus, but I've had consistent luck these last six months, and have sent twelve hundred dollars home.

I suppose you have read all about the new bill that Congress passed giving men who wear the expert combat badge an extra ten dollars a month. We were just told about it, and of course the news was well received, as we have all been awarded the medal and are entitled to the extra ten per. We have had the rating for almost six months now, and I'm wondering if we will get back pay. Time will tell.

Well, the beer rumor was true. We haven't had any as yet, but the stuff is nearby and it won't be long now. Twenty-four bottles a month is all we will be allowed, but that's not a bad beginning.

I'm surprised at you children. I thought that after the clues I gave you on SNAFU you wouldn't have any trouble figuring out what JANFU and CORFU mean, but I guess you're not on the ball. I won't keep you in suspense tho - JANFU when translated means "Joint Army Navy Foul Up." CORFU means "Commanding Officer Really Fouled Up." Catch on? The first letter of each word. Now see what you can do with TARFU and FUBAR and let me know the results.

Well, after a month of no shows, we are now seeing movies again. I just got in from tonight's show and I'm still in a happy frame of mind. The picture was Deanne Durbin in "Hers to Hold" and I thought it swell. I would still rather hear her sing than anyone I can think of. We had our first picture the other night. Loretta Young in "China." Although I had seen it once before, I liked seeing it again. What with beer and movies, first thing you know a guy will forget all about wanting to come home - In a pig's eye he will!

I'll never stop wanting to get back home, but I'm beginning to doubt if I will. That is for some time to come. In spite of all the high-sounding talk, there is nothing happening and I'm getting a bit discouraged about it all. Things are almost back to normal now, and maybe something will pop one of these days.

Well guys - will have to say a hasty goodbye again-
It's almost time for lights out and I want to get this in
the morning mail. Will write again soon and until
then say "Hello" to everyone for me....

As ever,
Joe

August 20, 1944
Hi Gang,

Well, here I come again with the monthly letter. Seems like I've been taking advantage of you all along, but this is the first time I've dared to answer four of your letters with just one. I don't know how come, but I just can't seem to get caught up on my writing. I owe one to Milly, one to El, and four or five others, and as much as it bothers me there doesn't seem to be anything I can do about it. Just started to reread the four letters and the one of June 17th looks mighty familiar. I do believe I answered it, and if so, that makes it only three to one in your favor and makes me feel a little less of a heel. Now to go on to the one of July 13th - I know I've never answered it.

Enjoyed reading the clippings you sent very much. It was the first time I had read any of the details as reported to the outside world and they were pretty much as represented. I hope that answers your questions as to where and why.

Glad you reminded me of that money, as I have another piece which will add to your collection. I'll enclose it in this letter.

Well, to go on to the letter of the 23rd. You sure made the vacation at Phillips sound like manna from heaven. I imagine there was fishing without end now that so many of the fishermen are now no longer able to indulge. Janet said something in her last letter about Joy's going up for a few days angling. I wonder how the bass are running at Wandawega?

I guess the folks haven't been seeing much of the summer home lately. In fact, they said something about selling the place.

Suzy, you keep me chuckling with some of the cracks you make. For instance, you said you didn't intend to bowl this year as you would be getting plenty of exercise in the house and then you added "doing housework I mean." It wasn't meant to be funny, but knowing John as I do it got me to wondering if that's what you meant. Anyway, it got to my funny bone. I'm all for that good old exercise in the house. Housework, of course. What else would I be talking about?

Things have been so routine out here lately as to be almost boring. Conditions have improved considerably, that we have rated fresh meat several times lately. Makes me suspect every time they start passing out fresh meat. Haven't had our beer ration yet, and don't know when we will, but it shouldn't be long now.

Had a letter from home and they tell me one of the lads from the neighborhood just came home on rotation after only twenty months in this theatre. Stuff like that makes me want to blow my top as I can't see how those things can happen. Seems to me the men who have the longest service should be given exclusive priority. Wouldn't mind too much, except that I can't even see when or if I'll ever get back - Oh well, can't have everything.

Will have to say bye again now. The chow line is starting to show some sign of life and with all this fresh meat a guy can't afford to be late. Will write soon again-

As always,
Joe

Timeline of the 158th Regimental Combat Team
September – December 1944

September-December 1944

The Bushmaster's enjoy some quiet time in recaptured Noemfoor before leaving for the Philippines.

September 4, 1944

Hi Gang,

Seems like no amount of trying on my part is quite up to keeping up with the mail. I've got two of your letters that have been crying for an answer for almost a week, and this is the first opportunity I've had to do anything about it. However, I will follow your wishes and refuse to apologize for not writing more often.

Well guys, all sorts of news since my last letter, but nothing of any real importance. Still working pretty hard, but it is much more pleasant work than some of the labor we have been doing recently, so no one minds very much. The only trouble with this routine work is that it becomes very dull in a short time and first thing you know you find yourself wishing for new pastimes.

It was just a month overdue, but at long last the much-promised beer has arrived. Tomorrow is the big day and we rate ten bottles per man, which is a pretty good beginning. We have been trying to figure out ways and means of getting the stuff fairly well cooled off, but so far no one has come up with a workable idea.

*Remainder of letter is missing

September 16, 1944

Hi Gang,

Get a load of this stationery. Next letter will probably be written on an old shirt tail or a roll of tissue. Had your letter of August 26th and it was delivered in damn near record time. I hope the service keeps up the good work.

Got a bit of gossip for you this letter in regards to our favorite subject-rotation. Seems like the people of Arizona (you know that the outfit came from that state) have been kicking up a bit of a fuss because of our being so long overseas with no relief. It was finally brought to the attention of the Governor and State Senator and I understand they have asked for a public investigation. Probably won't ever come to a thing, but there is always the chance that it may do some good.

Looks now like I will get a furlough to Sydney long before I get home on rotation. In fact, I should get the furlough within a few months - I'm going to hate taking it because I had my heart set on coming home, but damned if I turn it down. Life's too uncertain in this neck of the woods.

I wonder if you have seen the picture that was released by the army entitled "Attack". If not, be sure to look it up and see it. I found it very interesting, possibly because we had a part in the making. It has to do with the invasion of New Britain, and believe me it's the real McCoy.

We are having a sort of a celebration over the next weekend on the occasion of the fourth-anniversary of the outfit's being inducted into federal service. Won't be much - just all sorts of athletic competitions and

Saturday nite a beer bust. We have been saving our rations and with luck we'll have six bottles per man.

One of the fellows got some pictures the other day, and since I make a brief appearance, I thought you might like to see them. They're quite old, having been taken on New Britain, but it takes that long to get them developed.

Had a letter from Brownie yesterday and talking about fast service - it was only fifteen days en-route. Considering that it has always taken at least two months, that is plenty fast. He is still well and not complaining.

Well gang, will have to say bye until later. Say "Hello" to everyone for me and write soon...

As ever,
Joe

September 24, 1944 (written on American Red Cross stationery)

Hi Gang:

The early part of this week was certainly quite dull in so far as the mail clerk was concerned. He just went his merry way with never a letter for poor old me and then he must have had an attack of guilty conscience or something, because he certainly made up for his neglect over the weekend by swamping me with letters. That's a long way around to say that I got some mail isn't it? Anyhoo, your letter of Labor Day was among those received, and it was sure good hearing from you again.

Believe it or not, your mentioning Labor Day reminded me that there still was such a thing as holidays. Don't suppose it meant much to the folks back home (at least not to you) and it certainly didn't mean a thing to us except a day of labor. In fact - I had completely forgotten about it and I guess the rest of the boys did too.

Had a letter from Brownie and it seems the boy is doing well for himself. He sent a picture of himself and he really looks good. Doesn't seem to have changed a bit except that he has lost some weight which if anything makes him look better. Also heard from the big fella and talk about a gravy train -he is really on one. He just returned from furlough and to listen to him tell about it, it was no slow leak. He spent the time driving through California seeing the sites and doing all sorts of fishing from trout to deep sea. Don't know how he does it, but I'm glad to know that someone in this army gets a break occasionally. My own viewpoint on the subject is so warped that I can't see how, but evidently those things do happen.

Last time I wrote you I had myself all kidded into thinking that I would soon get a furlough to Australia. Even went so far as to have the folks send me some money. Well, might have known that the bubble would burst. I should have known better, but I have reached the stage where I will grasp at any straw. Anyway, it all turned out to be just wishful thinking and right now I am as far away from going somewhere as ever. The old morale is getting pretty shaky and sometimes I wonder when it's going to break completely down. They don't want human beings in this army-what they want is a bunch of supermen.

Got some more pictures that I was intending to send in this letter, but no soap-they haven't been passed and stamped by the base censor so I will have to send them back to base before sending them to you - probably will take at least a month.

Also heard from Joy and Janet, and Janet said something about all of you going to see the picture that was released by the army signal corps called "Attack."* They showed it to us not long ago and it is certainly well worth seeing. Didn't recognize my face, but we did have a part in the making of it. One thing about it, there was nothing Hollywoodish about it. If you haven't seen it yet, don't fail to do so.

So, Tony has decided to go into the tavern business. One nice thing about it, it will simplify the problem of finding John when you want him. I might add that goes for yours truly when he gets there.

We have been enjoying some very pleasant weather this past week. In fact, pleasant everything. Have been doing lots of work, but not too much. We're seeing a *show every other night. Saw a little piece by the name of "Cairo" last night and it wasn't bad.*

Well kids, I hate to be so brief but really must sign off for now. Still have the rest of those letters to write and it's getting later than I thought. Will write soon I promise and until then....

My best to everyone,
Joe

*The film, "Attack: The Battle for New Britain", is still available on Amazon.

September 30, 1944
Hi Gang:

There is something wrong in your apologizing for not writing more often, when it's definitely I who hasn't been on the ball lately. I haven't an excuse to offer either. Just one of those depressing moods when nothing seems right and every time I start to write a letter, I wind up staring into space and finally end up by letting it go until tomorrow. We have been on the gravy train lately. I've been averaging one six-hour detail a day and the rest of the time to do with as I please. Usually a bridge game. I have been in this "don't give a damn mood too long." Seems as though these moods have been coming oftener staying longer than used to be, but the future has so little in store that just thinking about it is enough to give you the willies. I don't know how those things start Suzy, but this business of expecting me home in the near future is definitely off the track. I know it's mostly my fault, because I'm always writing about it and no doubt giving the wrong impression. It's about time I started to act my age and forget this indulging in daydreaming. There doesn't seem a chance of getting back before war's end. Hell, might as well forget the whole thing.

I wonder if you have heard the latest of the Roosevelt-Churchill stories-? Seems like the last time Winnie was in Washington, Roosevelt caught him coming out of Eleanor's room. He said "See here I don't want any more of that." Churchill replied, "Me either." Well, I thought it was funny.

Should be having a payday most any day now and then the poker games will take the place of bridge for at least a few days. They picked me last month and I'll have to get it back from them this trip.

Went to the show last nite in the fond hope of seeing what I thought would be a good picture. It was "The Hairy Ape" and all I can say is it will probably take a week to get the bad taste out of my mouth. Of all the "stinkers" I've seen, that one does take the cake. Phooey!

A couple of us went over to the strip yesterday - just moseying around looking at the planes and talking to the pilots and crews and I've all but talked myself into going on a mission with them one of these days. Don't know yet whether I can get permission, but I'm hoping to work it out somehow. I sure would like to make a trip. Will let you know how it all comes out.

Fraid I'll have to cut this short. It's just about time to change clothes and go to work again. In fact, it's past time so I'll have to hurry. Give my best to everyone huh, and I'll be seeing you. ...

Hastily,
Joe

211

Netherlands, East Indies
October 24, 1944
Hi Gang,

I guess I've really got it coming to me this time. It's been so long since my last letter. Have had very few opportunities for writing these last three weeks and even when the time was to be had, something always seemed to come along. We have been (and still are) in the middle of a terrific paper drought and there just isn't any stationery to be had. If something doesn't happen to end the shortage, my next letter will probably be written on the good old musical roll.

Spent some time doing outpost and patrol duty since my last letter, but am now back at base camp again going thru the same old routine. Just got back from a ten mile hike a few hours ago and am now trying to nurse my barking pups and write this letter all at one time. You really have to be in the best of shape to take that walking in this heat, so I must be pretty fit for my age.

Oh yes! Had another issue of beer since I last wrote. Six cans of Miller High Life this time. Still leaves us 21 bottles for this month, which I doubt we will get.

I'll bet you're thinking this long time between letters means that I'm either in Australia on furlough or on my way home. Wish either one of them were the case, but still nothing doing. In fact, the furlough seems to be out once and for all. As for rotation, the less said about that SNAFU the better.

No doubt you have heard all about the landings in the Philippines. We all think it's the best news yet. Sort of hoped to be on it, but that wasn't to be. Oh well, no doubt I'll get my chance. Will have to close now as this is all the paper I have. Will write again as soon as I can get the paper. Still have lots to say. So, bye for now and give my best to everyone...

As always,
Joe

Netherlands, East Indies
November 20, 1944
Hi Gang,

I am certainly full of good intentions about writing letters, but as I have found out this past week, it takes more than good intentions when there is no spare time. I wish I were the type to keep a diary. A day by day record of what's happened to me these last three years would make good material for a book.

Had your letter of the 28th of October about a week ago and then yesterday the one of the 10th of November. Incidentally, the latter made really remarkable time. I find it hard to believe, but the postmark doesn't lie.

Lordy, gal, when you start asking questions you don't fool. Such a curiosity, tsk-tsk. Wish I could answer all of them, but I'm afraid those queries in regards to Generals divisions will have to go unanswered for a while yet. As to the others, I'll do the best I can.

I'm surprised that you don't know what is meant by "the strip". Johnny should know the answer to that one. It's just the vernacular for the place the planes land on. In other words, the airfield. And speaking of the strip, I'm still without that promised plane ride. No fault of the boys who promised it-just haven't had the time as yet. I'll be going over one of these days tho.

About radio programs - we have a pretty good set over at the chaplain's tent and it's available to all who care to go over. I guess we hear most all of the big programs by rebroadcast, although I very seldom listen to anything but the news.

I guess I do know what you meant when you said I would understand about John and Janet's arguments in regards to Roosevelt and Dewey. She has had something to say about the election in all of her recent letters and I did my share of needling in my answers. She can't very well hang up the phone on me via letter, but I'll bet she would have, had she had the chance. The news of the election was received out here with very little display. No one seemed to care particularly who was elected. I think they would rather hear just one little word about when this will be over and how long before we get back.

Did I tell you I am now a GI cook? Must sound funny to you. I know it does to me. It all came about when one of the boys in the kitchen went home on rotation and another to the hospital. I just sort of went in to help out and wound up a permanent fixture. Seems like a pretty good deal. We work one day on and one off, although it hasn't worked out that way yet. Last week, we off-duty cooks had to take a refresher course on the fifty-caliber machine gun, and as a result we were plenty busy all week.

Spent two days on the anti-aircraft rocket range and it was a new experience for yours truly. Lots of fun and I wish I could get more of it. Reminded me of the times we had on New Britain when we used to shoot at Zeros. One day we opened up on a Jap who was too far out of range to hit. We knew we didn't have a chance of hitting him, but thought it was a good excuse to fire the gun. Well, the upshot of it all was that we were called over to headquarters and had our little fannies chewed out by no less than the General. Believe me, after that we didn't shoot that thing unless we had a chance of hitting something.

Had a letter from home today and was surprised with the news that Mother and Ginny have taken off for a vacation in New York. Don't know what brought it about, but will no doubt get the details after they get back.

Well, another four days and it will be Thanksgiving again. I hear that the Q.M. (Quartermaster) has a turkey dinner with all the fixings for us, but haven't seen any of it yet. Probably won't be issued until the day before. Hell, the whole thing is just a mockery anyway. Holidays don't hold any meaning for us anymore. I don't care whether we have turkey or corn willy.

Did I tell you that we have a Red Cross canteen with us these days complete with two gal workers? We had them over for dinner the other day and did we ever go social.

After all of my vows not to get out on a limb again with rotation talk until something definitely turns up, here I go again. Now mind, there is nothing official about this, but the thing does look very promising again.

I have every reason to believe that I'll be sometime between now and April-getting home no later than June. Of course, that's mere conjecture, and as I said not official, but that's the way it will work out unless there are some drastic changes. It's still a long way to go, but after all the sweating I've done six months or so are a snap.

Well guys - will have to say bye for now. I really have to write a letter to El before calling it a day. Have had two from her and her latest informed me in no uncertain terms that I had better get on the ball. Can't argue with the gal, because she's right for a change. Will write again soon and until then
Love and Hello to all, Joe

Netherlands, East Indies
December 2, 1944
Hi Gang,

Well, it begins to appear that in spite of the fact that I now have every other day off, I still can't keep up with you in this matter of letter writing. I had better get on the ball, because when I don't write now I can't offer any alibis as formerly.

Just finished the weekly family laundry, and it behooved me to get busy with pen and ink before a spell of laziness catches up to me, as it invariably does about one every afternoon.

Your letters of the 3rd and 17th of November both arrived safely, and need I say I was mighty glad to hear from you period. So very often letter writing becomes a drudge because of the limited number of things we are allowed to talk about, but never is that the case with you. That insatiable curiosity of Suzy's is always asking enough questions to make writing a letter an easy job. I make it sound as though it was a task, but I don't mean it that way at all.

Asked Hal about your friends, the resort owners, and he said that he had heard of them many times, but never had the pleasure of meeting them.

I won't request the paper as you asked me to do, because I don't think it would be worth all the trouble involved in getting it here. Now that we have a Red Cross canteen it is only a matter of a few moments' walk to replenish the supply and why put you to any trouble. Chances are that were you to send some they would get manhandled, possibly soaked, and just be no good in general by the time it got to me. Thanks, anyhoo.

Have had a very quiet and routine week. Not a thing happened that wasn't commonplace. Worked Tuesday, Thursday, and Saturday and on off days just plain loafed. Have been using all of my free time in giving myself a course of home treatment, with the result that my legs are as good as new again. Mighty glad I am, because those damned tropical ulcers can be most annoying.

Don't know where John got the idea that I was holding out on the rotation, but it ain't so. It's as I told you in my last letter. That was the latest and there have been no changes. Don't worry - that's one secret I couldn't keep even if I wanted to.

Now about the matter of nicknames- I picked up the name "Jimmy" a long time ago and it stuck. It all started in Panama and was more or less in self-defense. Down there everybody and everything is called Joe. Bartenders, taxi drivers, just everybody and with the result that every time someone yelled, "Hey Joe" (which was almost every minute of the day) all of us poor birds who wore that handle would start to go crazy trying to find out what they wanted. Couldn't take it, so I became "Jimmy." Also, have had a few unpleasant handles due to my being from Chicago. I have always been a target for remarks, because I am the only one around here from Chi. But unpleasant as some of the things I am called might be, they are all in fun.

Had a luscious payday the other day. Finally got the extra combat pay. Ten months of it at ten bucks per, make it a nice bundle. Plenty of good poker games and I had my usual good run of luck. I don't know why, but for some reason I just can't seem to lose. Okay, once in a while I take a lickin', but in the

218

long run I always come out on top. Set one of the boys all in last night and wound up wearing his watch-cost me a hundred, but it's a damn good timepiece and well worth the money. If my luck turns sour I can always sell it for what I paid.

We have been seeing some rather good pictures this last week - much better than usual. Saw Ingrid Bergman in "Gas Light", also Red Skelton in "Bathing Beauty" and I liked both of them very much. Tomorrow night we expect to see Barbara Stanwyck in "Double Indemnity" and that too should be worth seeing.

Haven't had any packages come in for some time now, but there should be a deluge most any time now - When and if they get here there should be something for me. Must confess I am a little curious to see the inside of some of those packages, especially the miniature tree from my little chum. Almost forgot! Had a card from Tony and Laura the other day, but no address on it- what's the matter with the kids? Too busy to drop a line. Jump on "em" next time you see them.

Well guys- haven't said much, but took so long in saying it that it's almost time for chow. Well, still enough time to look at a couple of cards if I hurry. Will write again soon and till then give my best to everyone...

Love,
Joe

Thought you might like to see this long distance shot of me. The other pics still haven't come in but should be here soon   J

Timeline of World War II in the Pacific 1944

January 16-17, 1944
Japan begins counterattacks in southern New Britain. However, by the 17th, the Allies have secured Arawe and other southern parts of the island.

March 19, 1944
U.S. destroyers attack Wewak on the northern coast of New Guinea.

April 21-22, 1944
U.S. begins landings on the northern coastline of New Guinea. Sarmi, Wakde Island and Hollandia are attacked by a U.S. Naval Taskforce.

May 17, 1944
U.S. 41st and 6th Divisions land in northern New Guinea in the Wakde -Toem area, 200 miles west of Hollandia.

May 28, 1944
The 158th, 162nd, and 186th Regiments land on Biak off northwest New Guinea unopposed. They engage in a vicious battle as they advance toward an airstrip.

May 29, 1944
U.S. and Japanese tanks engage in battle at Biak. This was the first tank battle in the Pacific Theatre. The Japanese were defeated.

July 2, 1944
U.S. troops land at Noemfoor Island, off the coast of New Guinea.

July 14, 1944
Battleships attack Japanese positions around Aitape allowing land troops to advance along the northern New Guinea coastline.

August 17-20, 1944
Japanese resistance against the U.S. is futile on Noemfoor and Biak Islands.

October 20, 1944
The U.S. invasion of the Philippines begins. The U.S. 6th Army goes ashore near Leyte unopposed

October 21, 1944
The Japanese counterattack the Leyte landings and are defeated.

Part VI
The Philippines
1945

"No need for you to answer this. Daddy doesn't live here anymore."

THE LUZON CAMPAIGN

▨ = COMBAT AREAS

Map Courtesy of Arizona State University Library

Driving the Japanese out of New Guinea was certainly a major conquest for the Allies. MacArthur's promise now faced the final test, as the Philippines were the next stop on this sojourn. The Liberation of the Philippines began in mid-October 1944, when troops landed at Leyte in the southeastern Philippines. By December 1944, Leyte and nearby Mindoro Island had been secured. These acquisitions gave the U.S. two airfields from which they could launch strikes on the most populated and most important island, Luzon. Manila, MacArthur's ultimate destination, and the capital, was located there. MacArthur's plan was to initially land at the Lingayen Gulf on the northwest coast of Luzon. This location would allow access to roads and railways that led south to Manila. The distance from Manila would provide space for the large number of forces he intended to use. The Luzon Campaign was the largest of the Pacific War; it involved ten U.S. Divisions and five independent regiments, one of which was the 158th RCT.

The Bushmasters were enjoying some downtime in New Guinea after helping to recapture it from the Japanese. This calm interlude started to dismantle in late December 1944, when the Luzon Campaign called for their skills. They left Noemfoor for the Philippines to participate in the ultimate mission: fulfilling MacArthur's promise to free the Philippines. The Bushmasters travelled aboard the USS APA Leon, which was a comfortable, clean ship with bunks in single quarters and good food. Their war experience had taught them to enjoy these simple pleasures, because they wouldn't last long. They made one stop along the way for maneuvers off Japen Island in order to prepare for what lie ahead. Mid-January 1945, the 158th landed at Lingayen Gulf in Northern Luzon. Parts of the 6th Army had already established a beachhead, and they landed unopposed.

One of their first missions was to secure the Damortis-Rosario Road. Control of this road was vital for American advancement to Manila. The Bushmasters were prepared. At this time, the 158th had 4500 men among 3 battalions as well as the 147th Field Artillery. Luzon Task Force battleships and destroyers were also ready, if needed for support. Despite such preparations, great obstacles waited patiently for them. The first problem was that Army Intelligence had once again underestimated the number of Japanese forces. Much more troubling was the fact that the Japanese had occupied the Philippines unopposed for over three years. This time had allowed them to build networks of tunnels in dugout caves with camouflaged openings. Within these caves, soldiers could hide large artillery, capable of long-range destruction, stockpile food and supplies, and move undetected from place to place.

The Bushmasters' introduction to the Philippines only took a few days to rise to mayhem. As the 158th advanced inland with the goal of securing Rt. 3 and Rt. 11 along the Damortis-Rosario Road, they were not aware they were only six miles from the Headquarters of the Japanese 14th Army. Well-hidden in plain sight, the Japanese were able to ambush the 158th with a barrage of heavy artillery in a short time. Casualties from mostly the 1st Battalion of the 158th were strewn everywhere, and that day later became known as "Bloody Sunday". After almost three more weeks of heavy fighting, the 158th, along with 172nd Infantry and the 63rd Infantry were able to secure the junction of Rt.3 and Rt. 11. This victory allowed the Allies to advance to Manila without Japanese interference. The final number of casualties was staggering. The 172nd Infantry reported 30 dead and 150 wounded. The 63rd Infantry lost 40 men and had 270 wounded. The 158th RCT lost 87 soldiers with 397 wounded. The Japanese death count was over 1000.

Once again, the 158th moved on. Company G was under the command of Captain Bayard W. Hart, a full-blooded Cherokee Indian. In early February 1945, Company G was in pursuit of an enemy patrol. They settled in for the night in an area near Cataguintingan. Without warning, they were jolted by the sound of a 30 CM Howitzer. They soon realized they were in close proximity to one of the largest enemy artillery pieces in the Philippines. This gun could send a 1300 lb. shell more than 9 miles away. When fired, it created a crater that could be as large as 28 ft. across and 9 feet deep. The gun was well hidden under a makeshift native shack. The shack was on rails, and when it was rolled out, the gun was able to be wheeled out. Army Intelligence knew this gun existed, as it was wreaking havoc on the American advancement attempts in the Philippines, but had been unsuccessful at locating it even with air reconnaissance missions. With somewhat of a stroke of luck, Company G was able to finally locate this destructive menace. With the help of tank support, they were able to secure the gun, ending with a death toll of 164 Japanese vs. one wounded Bushmaster. The capture of this gun was extremely significant towards aiding the American advancement in the Philippines. Some historians note that it symbolized the end of Japanese might in the Pacific Theatre. Company G was awarded the Presidential Citation for their accomplishment.

By mid-February, the battle-weary 43rd Division, along with 158th RCT were replaced by the 33rd Division. The 33rd pressed on, recapturing Baguio by the end of April.

By February 3, 1945, the way to Manila was finally cleared. Troops advanced on Manila, and after fighting much resistance, they entered the city. Futile as it was, Japanese resistance continued for another month, devastating the city even more. Manila was officially liberated on March 4, 1945. The people of Manila were free again, but left with the realities of war. The recapture of Manila was a large win for the U.S., however, the Luzon Campaign still had some months to go.

Once Manila was secure, General Krueger, Commander of the 6th Army ordered the clearing of the area south of Manila. This action was carried out by the XIV Corps, consisting of the 1st Calvary Division, the 11th Airborne Division, and the 158th RCT. This group covered the Bicol Peninsula and were able to form a line from Laguna Bay at the northern edge of the peninsula all the way to Batangas Bay on the southern coast. Early March brought heavy fighting for the Bushmasters in the Batangas Province, southeast of Manila. Along with the 11th Airborne Division, their mission was to clear Batangas Bay in order to increase American shipping to the islands. They accomplished this by mid-March with the cost of 35 dead and 128 wounded. The XIV Corps was also successful in regaining a highway that went between Santo Tomas and Batangas. This mission was accomplished by the end of March. The 158th RCT then received orders to detach from the 11th Airborne, in order to prepare for an amphibious landing at Legaspi, located on the southeast coast of the Bicol Peninsula.

The 158th carried out orders, and on April 1, 1945, Easter Sunday, the Liberation of the Bicol Peninsula began. As the Marines were invading Okinawa, Japan, the 6th Army, along with the 158 RCT, invaded the Bicol Peninsula. The 158th landed under sniper fire and were able to advance 500 miles before their first roadblock. Although there was still much fighting involved, the Japanese troops at this point were mainly support troops, service troops, and escapees from Leyte after the American takeover. The 158th, with their battle experience, stood up well to these weary and less experienced soldiers. They saw their heaviest fighting on April 3, 1945, but by April 14, Legaspi had fallen to the Bushmasters.

In early May, they were joined by the 1st Calvary Division, and by months end, all of Luzon was free of the enemy, and the XIV Corps was relieved. The Luzon Campaign cost the 158th twenty-five percent of its men. In the end, 226 were killed, 20 missing, and 1046 wounded. By the end of June, the Philippines were declared to be secure, and on July 5, 1945, MacArthur announced that all the Philippine Islands were liberated.

It became quite clear to anyone who served in the Philippines in 1945, that the Japanese had been instilling horrors on the Philippine people since their occupation in 1942. Documents later revealed that civilian murders were part of a calculated goal to exterminate the Philippine people. It has been estimated that even in their last few days of occupation, the Japanese army mercilessly killed over 100,000 citizens.

On the other side of the world, Germany was showing signs of defeat. Hitler committed suicide on April 30, 1945, and Germany surrendered on May 7, 1945. Although Japan was also nearing defeat, their code of honor would not permit surrender. Now that the Philippines were free of Japanese control, the only stop left on this tour of madness was Japan itself.

Okinawa was the first target for the Allies in Japan. Okinawa is an island south of the mainland. Located halfway between Formosa and Kyushu, Okinawa was a strategic start for the U.S. The Marines invaded Okinawa in April 1945, just as the Bicol Peninsula was invaded by the 6th Army. Fighting lasted over two months, and claimed the lives of 12,000 Americans and over 100, 00 Japanese. True to their custom, Japan refused to surrender.

After Okinawa, orders were written for the further invasion of Japan. They intended for the Bushmasters to perform a frontal assault on the island of Kyushu. Commanding officers knew that this was likely to be a suicide mission. Thankfully, those orders never came to fruition.

The Allies called for the unconditional surrender of Japan in late July, threatening "prompt and utter destruction" if Japan did not comply. Japan refused, and the war continued, but only for a short while longer. On August 6, 1945, an atomic bomb was dropped on the city of Hiroshima. Japan continued their refusal to surrender. Three days later, on August 9, 1945, an atomic bomb was dropped on Nagasaki. On August 15, 1945, Japan announced its surrender to the Allies.

A Japanese delegation formally signed the instrument of surrender aboard the USS Missouri on September 2, 1945, marking the official end of World War II.

Timeline of the 158th Regimental Combat Team
December 1944 – January 1945

December 29, 1944
Bushmasters leave Noemfoor, New Guinea aboard the USS APA Leon headed for the Philippines.

January 2, 1945
They stop for maneuvers off the coast of Japen Island in order to prepare for the next attack.

January 9, 1945
They enter Lingayen Gulf with little opposition. Assault troops of the 6th Army had already established a beachhead. Initial mission of the 2nd Battalion is to attack north along Highway 251 to Rabon, and to establish a post at Bani, where patrols could be sent north to the town of Damortis and northeast to Damortis-Rosario Road.

January 12, 1945
The 2nd Battalion captures Rabon. Company G pushes on to Bani and sends out patrols. One of the patrols discovers and destroys 150 tons of ammunition and 4 Japanese field pieces in the Demortis railroad station.

January 13, 1945
The 2nd Battalion captures Damortis. Company G continues to Namonitan to establish a roadblock. The remainder of the 2nd Battalion sets up a perimeter on high ground east of Damortis. The 3rd Battalion encounters a heavy Japanese presence just east of Bani and is unable to advance.

January 14, 1945
The 1st Battalion suffers high casualties as they move along the Damortis-Rosario Road. This day became known as "Bloody Sunday".

January 18-21, 1945
Battle of Blue Ridge

January 24-26, 1945
Battle for the Cataguintingan Ridge

January 27, 1945
The junction of Rt. 3 and Rt. 11 on the Damortis-Rosario Road is cleared for American advancement to Manila.

*This timeline explains why there is a gap in Joe's letters from
 December 2, 1944 to February 16, 1945

Timeline of the 158th Regimental Combat Team
February 1945 – May 1945

February 15, 1945
The 158th is relieved by the 33rd Division, and is put on reserve and sent to Tarlac for a rest.

February 16, 1945
Joe writes his first letter since December 2, 1944.

March 4, 1945
The Bushmasters arrive in Balayan, Batangas Province.

March 5, 1945
They begin an offensive to open Balayan and Batangas Bays.

March 12, 1945
Along with parts of the 11th Airborne Division, the 158th is involved in heavy fighting.

March 14, 1945
After almost two weeks of heavy combat, both bays are open for American shipping. The Bushmasters have lost 45 lives and the Japanese have lost 781.

March 25, 1945-June 15, 1945
The 158th is attached to XIV Corps, along with the 1st Calvary Division and the 11th Airborne Division.

Late March 1945
The 158th is ordered to prepare for an assault on Legaspi area, located on the Bicol Peninsula on the southeastern tip of Luzon.

April 1, 1945
The Liberation of the Bicol Peninsula begins as the 158th carries out an amphibious assault on Legaspi. They advance 500 miles without interference.

April 3, 1945-late May 1945
The Bushmasters engage in combat at Sorsogon, Camalig, and Mt. Isarog.

May 30, 1945
Luzon Campaign officially ends.

February 16, 1945 (the day after the 158th was relieved from
fighting along Damortis-Rosario Rd.)

Philippine Islands

Hello Gang,
   Yes, I know I've got the devil coming to me for this
apparent neglect, but it has been impossible to find
time for letters as I think you will understand. Life
hasn't been exactly that of Riley this last month and
whenever I did have a few moments to spare, I
invariably dropped off to sleep on the spot. Haven't
had very many moments like that tho. Things have
eased up for us now and I should be able to find a
little more time for things in the future. Guess maybe I
just told a little white lie, because I did have some
time day before yesterday and used it for going to
town. Again, I think you will understand, since it was
the first time I've "gone to town" in two years. I call it
that for lack of a better name- actually it consisted of
going into a nearby village and walking about. We
did have all the fried chicken and eggs we could eat
and also managed for a bottle of rum and a fifth of
gin. Nothing much when judged by the "good old
day," but it was certainly a treat to us after the hell
we have been having. These people are the friendliest
I've ever known. They will do anything asked of them
and ever since we have stopped here our laundry
(which has always been a headache) has not been a
thing to worry about.
   The mail service is steadily improving - (at least the
incoming mail) and should be back to normal very
shortly now.
   Have been hearing from you regularly and have
now the sum of four letters from you- all waiting for

234

an answer. I hardly realized it's been that long since I last wrote. Well anyway I'll just skim over lightly. First, the Christmas packages are still among the missing. We have had no parcel mail for over two months now, but I hear that there will be some soon. Will let you know when and if the packages arrive.

So you had an idea that I might be on my way back when you failed to hear from me. Well you were partially correct as it did involve a sea voyage and we are geographically closer to home now than when we started, but as for getting back home- that will have to wait another couple of months. It won't be too much longer now. Keep your fingers crossed for me, huh?

Did I tell you about the sea voyage?

*Missing following pages

*We can surmise that the missing pages included a description of Joe's voyage on the USS APA Leon, where they enjoyed private bunks, clean conditions, and good food.

February 22, 1945

Hello Gang,

Well, in spite of my promises I still am having a hard time trying to get off a letter to you. I know that I don't have to offer any excuses, but I would like you to know the why and where for whenever I don't write regularly. Happily, this last long break between letters wasn't occasioned by the doings of the Nips, but rather because we have been pretty busy building another camp. Yes, we were finally relieved and are now leading a life that is definitely on the peaceful side. Course, there is plenty to do and all the work will soon be caught up (I hope) and then there will be more time for going to town, etc.

I have three letters of yours around and I can't for the life of me recall whether I answered any of them. Anyhoo, the latest arrived yesterday and was your first addressed to the new APO. I gather from it that you hadn't as yet received my first letter to you at the time of writing it, but rather had gotten the address from the folks when they called you. I wrote to you only a few days after writing to them and I'm certain you have had the letter by now.

We finally had that long-expected package call.

*Missing following pages

April 1, 1945   (Liberation of Bicol Peninsula begins)

Hello Gang,

Well, here I am again and about time too. These long lapses between letters must be stretching your understanding almost to the breaking point, but honestly guys we have been that busy again. As a matter of fact, I had to come into the hospital to find the time for this letter, but more of that later. Thank the Lord that the incoming mail has been steady. It always is nice to hear from you even though I sometimes neglect you for weeks. Have had four letters from you these past two weeks and probably would have had more except that I came into the hospital five days ago and they haven't gotten around to forwarding my mail as yet.

Have heard too much on the subject of baggage and the possibility of my getting home along with it. Janet, you and the folks all commented on it and the whole thing evidently started with the folks having a misunderstanding about that card they received. Before the thing gets too far out of hand, let me explain how it all started. The baggage is nothing more than the few personal articles I had to leave behind when we left Australia two years ago. The army has only just now gotten around to forwarding this stuff home and that's the story in a nutshell. As for my coming back-well, there hasn't been time to think of rotation these last three weeks and so far as I know the situation is still unchanged. With a little luck I should get rotated either in June or July. Without that little luck (and that's the way it probably will be) I'll make it sometime at end of summer. In the meantime, there is the much more important job of staying alive until that day comes and that job is becoming more and more of a problem every day. Things should be coming back to normal soon now (at least for us) and I'm hoping we get a period of rest that will last long enough to see me through. You can never tell about that though. I believe it was in my last letter that I told you that we were building camp and taking it easy and look how long that lasted- about three days and we were off to the races again.

We have been getting the news from Europe and I don't see how that can last very much longer. I wouldn't be surprised to see it end most any day. I suppose it would make a big difference to us out here if everything were sent to us although we have been doing pretty good as is.

I was surprised to hear about Sig Levy - you didn't say, but I gathered that he is once again a civilian. I'll bet he is tickled pink to have it all behind him. Say "Hello" to him for me should you see him. Believe I remember Matty. Fact is, I know I do. Didn't he and his wife live somewhere in the vicinity of Irving Park Boulevard and Sheridan?

Now about this being in the hospital. It's nothing very serious. Just a mess of tropical ulcers on my legs have been giving me a lot of trouble. Spent some time trying to clean them up in the company, but living in the field the way we have been doing makes this job next to impossible. Most of the time it's a problem to find enough drinking water and consequently it's pretty hard to keep clean and those damned ulcers thrive on dirt. They finally sent me to the hospital and after only five days of treatment, they are practically gone. I don't come into a hospital but once every two years so while I'm here this time I'm going to have them look into another ailment of mine and see if I can't get it cured too. Tell you about that next letter.

Will say bye for now as I see the doctor at the other end of the ward starting his inspection. Haven't had time for a letter to Joy and Janet or to Eleanore, so won't you call them and explain? Tell them I'll write within a very few days. Will try to write more regularly in the future. I promise. So bye again till later. Write soon....

As always,
Joe

Philippine Islands
May 11, 1945
Hello Gang,

I'm hoping that by the time you receive this, you will have had a phone call from the folks explaining in part this once again long-delayed letter.

Have been back with the company a few days, previous to that I was too much on the move to manage a letter. Found upon my discharge from the hospital, that the outfit had moved a considerable distance from where I left them and that it would have involved some travelling to get back to the roost. Went to a casual camp to await transportation and after much finagling around they arranged another airplane ride, and so back to the company. Got back just in time to get in on the tail end of another caper and have been on the move ever since. Looks very much as though things will settle back to normal very shortly now and then it should be peaches and cream until I get called up for rotation. Found that while I was gone, they had sent another bunch home and were preparing to send still another. Fact is there are now so few of us old timers left that I felt like a stranger when I came back to what has been my home for almost four years. Rotation of the old personnel plus combat loss have certainly brought about a lot of change this past year. Found five weeks back mail waiting for me and the stack seems to be a foot high. Don't know how long it's going to take me to answer all those letters, but I'm gonna give it the old college try today and see just how far I can get. Incidentally, there were 6 letters from you dated March 13th to April 27th. It sure was manna from heaven for this letter starved GI. There certainly have been events a plenty since my last letter to you. First, the death of the President and then the end of the war in Europe. About Roosevelt, the news was of course a shock. I at first refused to believe it, made me think for the first time (as it must have made a lot of folks at home too) of the man who was to take his place. FDR was such a fixture, that no man could replace him and not seem dim by comparison. Truman seems to have gotten off to a good start; let's hope he keeps it up. The end of the war in Europe was of course the news of the century, considering how much it will mean to them eventually. The boys out here seem to be very matter of fact about it all. Had a letter from Brownie that evidently was written before they opened the final drive in Italy and he seemed rather discouraged. I'll bet the boys over there are singing a different tune now. A few of us got together the other day and started to add up our points. I suppose you've read about the system the army has devised for the discharge of a certain number of men on a point credit rating. What with the time in the army, time overseas, combat credit and all the rest, I've got way over a hundred points. There are damned few GIs that even come close to that total, so it's just possible I may get discharged as surplus after I get back to the States. It's something to think about anyway. I presume you've heard from the folks that the big fella is once again a civilian. Had a letter from him and he's tickled pink about it all. I guess he'll make his home in California, the climate and the fishing seem to agree with him. Did I ever tell you that G Company was awarded the Presidential Citation? Don't think I did, but it's official and no longer a secret. Our company was the only one in the regiment to be cited, proving again that it is the hardest of all citations to earn. In all modesty, we did earn it. They had a couple of openings in the kitchen when I got back, so I am once again a cook of sorts, this time for the duration of my stay overseas, I hope. Won't make any difference when I get back as I will be reassigned after my furlough and will probably wind up driving a truck in the air core or quartermaster. Had quite a few letters from Janet, the latest of which gave me the news of Joy's impending induction. I suppose it came too late to affect him, but I'm hoping the end of the European war will change his status and defer him permanently. Seems like there will be plenty of younger single men to fill the gaps now that we're fighting only the Nips.

Well guys, we'll make with the goodbyes again, am still hoping to write to El, Milly, Joy, and Janet today, but I'm beginning to doubt that I will get that far. Write soon huh.

As always,
Joe

May 29, 1945 (the day before the official end of the Luzon Campaign)

Hello Gang,

You guys with your telephone calls every time one of you gets a letter from me are making it harder and harder for your daddy to compose a letter. For example, I wrote to the folks and to Joy and Janet the other day so most anything I say in this letter will be old news when you finally get it. Well, maybe not as bad as all that, but you know what I mean.

Thought that I had finally managed to catch up with all that mail that was waiting for me when I got back from the hospital, but not so. I've got three more from youse guys, one from Milly and also one from El. Should get caught up my next day off tho - I sure hope so.

Making it just a bit harder to write a letter is the fact that not a damn thing has happened since the last time I wrote. We are still in the field, but things have been very quiet. We're plucking up an occasional Nip or two now and then, but that's nothing to get excited about. They are pretty much beaten up and going out after them is just like going out rabbit or duck hunting back home. Our rest camp is being rapidly completed and as soon as it is finished we will probably go out of action. I haven't seen it yet, but some of the fellows who have tell me that the place is not bad at all. It will be the first time that we ever moved into a completed camp.

I see where you have read all about the point credit system whereby the army is going to discharge a certain number of us old fogies. Naturally, it is one of the chief topics of conversation among those of us who are still left of the original outfit. The other day we were told that we would have to see a movie that had to do with the plan. It was an official War Department film and went into great detail about how it will work. They didn't tell us anything that we didn't already know, but it was official and that should stop a lot of these impossible rumors that have been making the rounds. We have already had our cards filled out and forwarded onto a higher headquarters, so it's just possible there will some sudden action one of these days. They say that the men with the most points will be the first to be discharged and if so, I will be one of the very first. I've got way over a hundred points and that's official. Oh well, it shouldn't be too long now before we know for certain. In the meantime, there is still rotation and I'm almost at the top of that list too. Makes a rosy picture doesn't it?

Will have to close for now - it's almost time for lights out and tomorrow is the "On" day so I had better get a bit of shuteye. Will write again soon...

As always,
Joe

Haven't been able to get any news on the doings of The Cubs and Sox so send me a few clippings, huh? Also put a few air mail stamps in you next letter - postage is getting scarce. J.

July 7, 1945
Luzon, P.I.
Hello Gang,

Well, it's been a long time in coming but the great day has at last dawned upon yours truly. Just heard the news officially and thought you would be interested in hearing it too. For myself and the rest of the boys who will be coming back with me- Well, we're as nervous as the shady lady on her first visit to church. I still find it hard to believe, but can find no reason for disbelieving so I guess this is it.

Don't know yet just when we will leave but it will be very shortly now. I should be well on my way by the time this letter reaches you. Have heard that there is a good chance of flying back, and if so that would be the best yet, but probably nothing will come of it.

Not having much luck in writing this. The boys are all gathered around discussing what they are going to do and I have to put my two cents into the argument too.

Will say bye for now and be seein' you.

As ever,
Joe

Will keep the folks posted as best I can and they will let you know what gives- No need for you to answer this. Daddy doesn't live here anymore.

J

My Dad

I knew very little about my dad's war experience. I knew he was in the jungles, but I never dreamed he *actually* fought in combat. In my mind, I told myself he was probably the cook and he stayed back and cooked for the guys as they went off to fight. Even as an adult, when I first discovered my dad and his unit, Company G, were awarded a Bronze Star, I still believed they gave him one because he was in the unit, not because he was in on the action.

The reason for this thinking is simple. First, my young mind could never have fathomed the realities of the war my dad experienced. Second, and most obvious, was the fact that my dad was a kind and gentle man. The kind of kind and gentle that fits the expression, "He wouldn't hurt a fly." My dad in a position of killing or being killed? Preposterous!

Learning, and eventually, understanding what my dad endured has brought me to tears many times. As I researched and the story became clearer to me, so did things my dad said and did when I was a kid. He hated the thought of camping, claiming he "had enough camping to last a lifetime." I had no clue. He wasn't deeply religious, but whenever someone was in a tight situation he would say "I never met an atheist in a foxhole." He also had a daily reminder of the jungle the rest of his life. I remember my dad's feet were always peeling. Always. He called it athletes' feet, but now I know it was the long-term effects of jungle rot. He also hated loud noises and had ringing ears. It makes sense why going to the fireworks with my dad on the 4th of July never happened. My father's disdain of the Vietnam War and his not liking guns also carried new meaning.

I remember one specific incident that in retrospect, was my dad probably having an episode of PTSD. I was about 12 when my dad came home after witnessing and helping a girl who was hit by a car while riding her bike. He knew just what to do and kept her calm while waiting for an ambulance. Unfortunately, by the time he returned home he was very sick and distraught. I had never seen him in such a state, and it scared me. It was like he had gone through a war or perhaps, to be more precise, he was reliving one.

247

My dad was a sentimental guy. He adored his daughters, nieces and nephews, and grandchildren. He had an endearing nickname for everyone he cared about.

My dad was fun loving and had great sense of humor. Born and raised as the oldest son of Hungarian immigrants on the north side of Chicago, he always had a passion for the city. He loved poker with the boys, volunteered in his community, and was especially passionate about Chicago sports teams. He always had an opinion on the trades, the players and the management. Whenever a Chicago sports controversy happened, Joe was the guy whose opinion everyone wanted. He loved to read, and he read four newspapers a day. He always enjoyed good food. I'm sure four and a half years in the jungle eating army rations fueled this appreciation.

My dad always told me December 7th changed his life twice. Once for the worst and once for the better. We all know one was Pearl Harbor, but years later, December 7th was also the day I was born. That day in 1941 was certainly life changing for him: and now that I know his story, it has new meaning for me.

My grandmother had a thick Hungarian accent and occasionally she would say, "Your fatha vas a var hero and he von medals." He would always cut her off and say, "Oh ma, quit telling stories." I didn't know about the Bronze Star when he died, but I now know it should have been there right by his coffin. Perhaps it was meant to be that way; he would never want the attention or recognition.

My dad died in 1987 at the age of 72. He was too young, and looking back, I wonder if his brutal war experience robbed him of a longer life. The hard work in the jungle, constant exposure to disease, mental anguish, battle fatigue, unrecognized PTSD, the list could go on. I believe these had to have some effect on his longevity.

That old blue suitcase that started this mission became what my cousin and I fondly nicknamed "The Holy Grail", a three-ring notebook holding my dad's story in the form of 99 letters. Organizing those mostly undated letters in chronological order was a lengthy labor of love for my cousin and me. We laughed and cried all the way, but mostly we were in awe of the man we called father and uncle.

248

My dad, like so many others, came back from the war, glad to be alive, just wanting to return to the life they fought so bravely to protect. They never talked about their experience, at least not to family. I grew up never knowing what my dad went through in the war. I know there are others like me, who never knew their loved one's story, or what they endured during this time. This project has been a window into my dad's life. I hope this story will spark other sons and daughters of my generation to explore the war experience of their WWII veteran.

Mary Jo

Timeline of World War II in the Pacific 1945

January 2-8, 1945
The 6th Army leaves Leyte and begins to position themselves off Lingayen Gulf near Luzon.

January 9, 1945
The Luzon Campaign begins. The 6th Army lands at Lingayen Gulf with minimum resistance. The Japanese purposely pull their troops back, in order to conserve them for later combat.

January 20, 1945
U.S. forces engage in heavy battle on the Island of Luzon, 100 miles from Manila.
Kamikaze pilots attack U.S. Naval vessels near Luzon. The USS Ticonderoga and USS Langley are badly damaged.

January 23, 1945
The Americans take Clark Field in southern Luzon. This field will be instrumental in forthcoming operations on Iwo Jima.

January 29-31, 1945
More U.S. troops land in Luzon, in order to position around Manila. The XI Corps goes ashore just north of the Bataan Peninsula. Troops also land south of Manila Bay. These positions allow a three-pronged assault against the Japanese holding Manila.

February 2, 1945
The U.S. surmises that Japanese shipping losses in the Pacific have come to more than 50 per week. More and more, Japanese maritime power is being eliminated.

February 3, 1945
The month-long battle for Manila begins. The Japanese answer the Allied advancement with a vengeance.

February 6, 1945
Allied POW's that were taken by the Japanese in Bataan in 1942 are freed, following an intense raid by U.S. Rangers and Filipino insurgents.

February 16-27, 1945
The island of Corregidor in the Philippines is re-occupied by U.S. troops.

February 19, 1945
Following months of air and naval bombardment, the U.S. land invasion of Iwo Jima begins. Iwo Jima is a small island approximately 750 miles south of Tokyo. The battle of Iwo Jima is the first battle to take place on the homeland of Japan. Recapturing this island was vital, because fighter planes and bombers could land there for further attacks on the Japanese mainland. Iwo Jima is one of the bloodiest battles in U.S. Marine history.

February 20, 1945
The first airstrip on Iwo Jima is taken by the U.S. There are two more on the island that still need to be conquered.

FDR and Winston Churchill shift priorities to the Pacific Theatre, since the defeat of Germany is eminent.

February 21, 1945
Another airfield on Iwo Jima is taken by the U.S.

February 22. 1945
The Japanese 14th Army is pushed back from Manila.
2000 Japanese soldiers on Corregidor commit suicide by detonating a large ammunition dump.

February 25, 1945
U.S. airpower attacks the Tokyo area.

February 27-28, 1945
The Bataan Peninsula is effectively cleared by Units of the XI Corps.

February 28, 1946
U.S. forces advance on the third airstrip on Iwo Jima, Motoyana Airstrip.

March 1-31, 1945
U.S. Forces invade the multiple islands of the southern Philippines. By months end, the Philippines are effectively in U.S. hands.

March 9-10, 1945
Tokyo, the capital of Japan, is nearly destroyed by U.S. bombers.

March 11, 1945
U.S. Marines take over most of Iwo Jima's east coast. This leaves Japan with only a small territory on the northern part of the island.

March 12-13, 1945
Osaka, Japan is decimated by 274 U.S. air bombers.

March 14, 1945
The U.S. flag is raised over Iwo Jima, however, futile Japanese resistance continues.

March 16-17, 1945
Kobe, Japan is raided by American B29 bombers.

March 21, 1945
USS Bismarck, which helped support the Philippine Campaign, as well as Iwo Jima, is sunk by Japanese Kamikaze pilots.

March 26, 1945
Japanese resistance on Iwo Jima finally ends. The battle for this five square mile island ends with U.S. losses at 6,821, while Japanese casualties are estimated at 22,000. All the islands in the southern Philippines are under U.S. occupation.

April 1, 1945
Operation Iceberg begins when the 10th Army starts to position for an invasion of Okinawa. The landings are unopposed; however, 130,000 Japanese soldiers are waiting for them in the interior of the island. Japanese propaganda instills great fear of U.S. soldiers among the citizens, and they begin to commit mass suicide rather than face the "cruelty" of U.S. soldiers.

Formal education for children above the age of 6 in Japan is cancelled in order to bring these youth into the Japanese labor force to support the war industries.

U.S. troops land at Legaspi on the southern end of the Bicol Peninsula in the Philippines.

April 3, 1945
U.S. Marines cross Okinawa, reaching the east coast, cutting off Japanese troops in the Katchin Peninsula.

April 5, 1945
Kamikaze pilots attack Okinawa rendering heavy damage to U.S. ships.

April 7, 1945
U.S. troops meet heavy resistance in southern Okinawa, however, Marines continue to make progress on the east and west coasts.

April 9, 1945
One half of the Motobu Peninsula is under U.S. control. More than 43,000 Okinawans come under U.S. protection.

April 12, 1945
President Roosevelt dies at the age of 63. Vice President Harry Truman assumes the presidency.

April 12-15, 1945
U.S. aircraft bomb four airbases in southern Japan, where U.S. troops have been struggling. 246 Japanese aircraft are destroyed.

April 13, 1945
U.S. Infantry and offshore naval firepower defeat a Japanese Battalion in southern Okinawa.

April 14, 1945
U.S. Marines make great advances in northern Okinawa.

April 21, 1945
The U.S. flag is raised on Ie Shima in the Rykukyu Islands.

April 29, 1945
U.S. Navy hospital ship, USS Comfort, is attacked by Kamikaze aircraft. 29 patients and crewmembers die, 33 are wounded, and 100 persons are missing.

May 5, 1945
17 U.S. ships are sunk by Kamikaze pilots off Okinawa.

May 13, 1945
U.S. air attacks begin over Kyushu, destroying Japanese railroad network and airfields.

June 21, 1945
The long bloody battle to capture Okinawa finally ends. The Americans are now in position to reach the shores of mainland Japan. The number of casualties on both sides is staggering.

July 5, 1945
General MacArthur announces that the Philippines are fully liberated.

Joe's Photo Album

PRETTY RUGGED LOOKING, ARENT THEY

CHORRERA FALLS

THAT'S ME AT THE GUN IN THE MIDDLE.

Joe on right (no caption)

GRAIG "BEN" HANNUM
TOP KICK OF G. COMPANY
LOOKS LIKE HE'S GOING
SOMEWHERE BUT HE WAS
JUST FOOLING.

"MACKINAW" EDSON AND MYSELF.

"MACKINAW" EDSON AND A G.I. TRUCK

Joe (no caption- possibly Texas)

WARRANT OFFICER
HOYER
BAND LEADER OF THE
REGIMENT

CHAPLAIN SAMSON
AGAIN

"Bow" Bowman From
Indianapolis on Left.
"Sleepy" Gibson From
Phoenix Arizona.

Two of The Best

238 THIS IS G. COMPANY
ON A SAFARI INTO THE
JUNGLE
5/19/42

THE CANTEEN AT CHORRERA

This caption has been typed for legibility:

From left to right (rear). Guess who?, "Fuzz" Bless, "Turtle" Bleak, "Bow" Bowman, "Red" McGrady.
Bottom Row "Jack" Jackson, "Chas" Hall.

MILITARY POLICE M.P.s To you
AND PLENTY TOUGH

"SLEEPY" GIBSON

"SLEEPY" GIBSON (CENTER)
"BENNY" VERRUE AND
3 - WHO?

SLEEPY AGAIN
"CHARLEY" CHARLEBOIS AND ME.

SGT "DOBBIE" ROBINSON
OF ARIZONA.

LT B.ll HART oF G. Co

No Comment.

989

272

"MACKINAW" EDSON ON TRUCK
HAROLD SIEFERT

A SPOT OF BVIDGE BETWEEN FIGHTS

THE KID IN THE FOX-HOLE IS
HAL SIEFERT - HE IS THE "CHEESE
MAKER" YOU ONCE ASKED ABOUT
NOTE THAT I HAUNT LOST THE
ART OF FINDING THE PRONE
POSITION

Tommy "MACKINAW" EDSON AND
ONE OF OUR COMPANY PETS

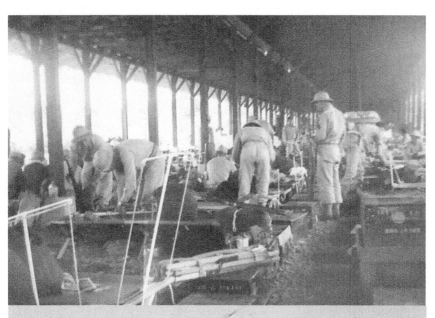

231 SPENT THREE HAPPY? DAYS
HERE ONCE UPON A TIME

277

IN LEFT FOREGROUND,
   LT ORVILLE COCHRAN.
      MY COMPANY COMMANDER THEY DON
   COMPANY BETTER.
(MIDDLE) LT CHRISTINI   SERVICE CO
(RIGHT) MAJOR GIBBS
   BATTALION EXECUTIVE OFFICER
(BACK) LT CARL BYAS
         CO G

"GUN CAPTURED BY "G" COMPANY - PHILLIPINES - 1945

Photo Courtesy of Arizona State University
Caption reads
Gun captured by "G" Company Philippines 1945

279

One of Joe's letters, very few were written on this type of stationary

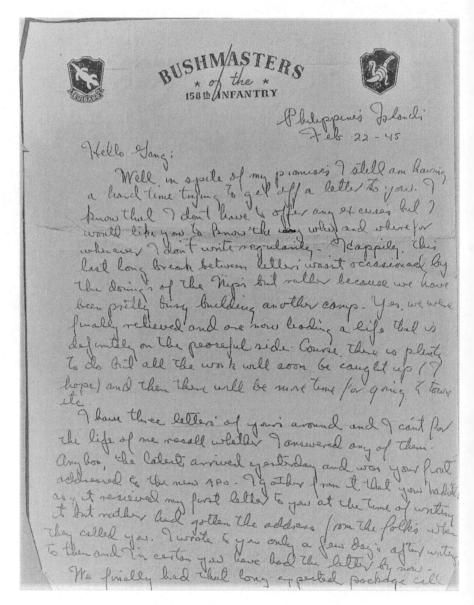

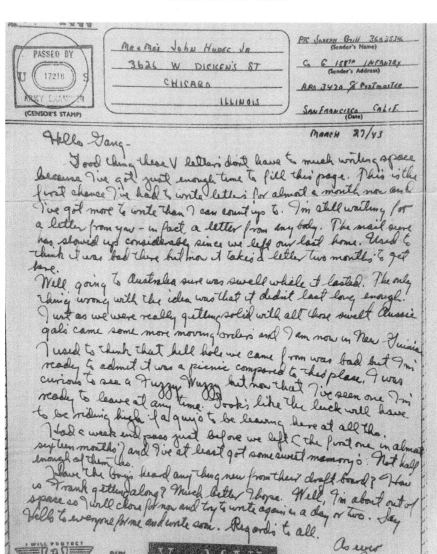

PASSED BY
U 17218 S
ARMY CENSOR
(CENSOR'S STAMP)

Mr & Mrs John Hudec Jr
3626 W. DICKEN'S ST
CHICAGO
ILLINOIS

PFC JOSEPH Brill 36035316
(Sender's Name)
Co G 158th INFANTRY
(Sender's Address)
APO 3420 % Postmaster
SAN FRANCISCO CALIF
(Date)

MARCH 27/43

Hello Gang-

Good thing these V letters don't have to much writing space because I've got just enough time to fill this page. This is the first chance I've had to write letters for almost a month now and I've got more to write than I can count up to. I'm still waiting for a letter from you - in fact, a letter from anybody. The mail sure has slowed up considerably since we left our last home. Used to think it was bad there but now it takes a letter two months to get here.

Well going to Australia sure was swell while it lasted. The only thing wrong with the idea was that it didn't last long enough! Just as we were really getting solid with all those swell Aussie gals came some more moving orders and I am now in New Guinea. I used to think that hell hole we came from was bad but I'm ready to admit it was a picnic compared to this place. I was curious to see a Fuzzy Wuzzy but now that I've seen one I'm ready to leave at any time. Looks like the luck will have to be riding high [a guy's] to be leaving here at all tho.

I had a week end pass just before we left (the first one in almost sixteen months) and I've at least got some sweet memorys. Not half enough of them tho.

Have the boys heard anything new from their draft board? How is Frank getting along? Much better I hope. Well, I'm about out of space so I will close [for] now and try to write again in a day or two. Say hello to everyone for me and write soon. Regards to all.

As ever
Joe

BUY
WAR BONDS
V-MAIL

281

THE UNITED STATES OF AMERICA

TO ALL WHO SHALL SEE THESE PRESENTS, GREETING: THIS IS TO CERTIFY THAT THE PRESIDENT
OF THE UNITED STATES OF AMERICA AUTHORIZED BY EXECUTIVE ORDER, 24 AUGUST 1962 HAS AWARDED

THE BRONZE STAR MEDAL

TO   PRIVATE FIRST CLASS JOSEPH H. BRILL, UNITED STATES ARMY

FOR   meritorious achievement in ground combat against the armed enemy
during World War II in the Asiatic-Pacific Theater of Operations.

GIVEN UNDER MY HAND IN THE CITY OF WASHINGTON
THIS   28th   DAY OF August   1996

THE ADJUTANT GENERAL

SECRETARY OF THE ARMY

Battles of the 158th Regimental Combat Team at a Glance

- December 1944 - Arawe, New Britain Island
- May 1944 - Wakde Island-Sarmi New Guinea opposed by crack 36th Tiger Division relieved by the 6th Infantry Division
- July 1944 - Amphibious assault Noemfoor Island, New Guinea
- January 1945 - Amphibious assault Lingayan Philippine Islands relieved by 33rd Infantry Division
- March 1945 - Batangas Province, Southern Luzon, Philippine Islands relieved by 11th Airborne Division
- April 1945 - Amphibious assault Legaspi Southern Luzon, Philippine Islands
- April 1945 - Amphibious assault Bacon, Sorsogen Province Philippine Islands
- April 1945 - Camalig, Cituinan Hill mass, Luzon Province, Philippine Islands
- May 1945 - Mt Isarog Bicol Peninsula, Philippine Islands

Fort Tuthill Museum website (www.forttuthill.org)

The 158th Regimental Combat Team wrote the book on 'Jungle Warfare' with its own blood. Any history written about the war in the Pacific would be incomplete if it failed to mention the many military exploits of the 'Bushmasters.' You have set records that will never be broken. The 158th served five and one-half years on active duty and was:

- Continuously in a combat zone longer than any National Guard unit in all U.S. wars.
- The first Army unit to be trained in jungle warfare establishing the first Jungle Warfare School.
- The first Army unit to be sent overseas after Pearl Harbor.
- The organization that traveled further in their 5 ½ years of active duty than any Army unit in any war.

Fort Tuthill Museum website (www.forttuthill.org)

An Army training report from March of 1943 describes the expectations for soldiers in jungle warfare.

"Each individual must possess superior physical fitness, initiative, resourcefulness and aggressiveness, the ability to make long marches, the ability to advance, attack, defend and maneuver in the jungle, individually and in small units; perfection in scouting and patrolling, and in use of cover and concealment; and the ability to operate in the jungle for considerable periods of time, conserving and using only his initial supplies and rations. Moreover, he must master the elements, learning how to prevent serious illness and ailments through his own application of preventative measures." The report concludes with "The Bushmaster is that kind of fighting man."

A 1943 article in *Popular Mechanics* magazine recorded the abilities of the individual Bushmaster jungle soldier:

"One of America's most colorful and least known soldiers of World War II is the Bushmaster. His tactics are borrowed from native jungle fighters, the American Indian, British commandos, exponents of judo and the Shanghai underworld. He uses machetes, curved knives, tommy guns, high-powered rifles, and hand grenades. His average age is 22 and his favorite weapon is the long-bladed machete. With his fellow Bushmasters, he disappears from civilization for weeks at a time. The men know how to sustain themselves on wild fare supplemented by jungle rations carried in their packs. When they are not testing their camouflage against aerial observers, making camp in a swamp, or working out an intricate code of communications, they are practicing jujitsu or improving on the natives' technique with the machete. The Bushmaster bows to no man in the art of hand-to-hand fighting and any unwary enemy who crosses his path would probably never know what hit him."

From John Vader, *New Guinea: The Tide is Stemmed, pp. 102-103*:

"In the swamp country which surrounded the area
(New Guinea) were large crocodiles. Incidence of malaria
was almost one hundred percent. At Sanananda the swamp and jungle
were typhus-ridden...crawling roots reached out into stagnant pools
infested with mosquitos and numerous crawling insects... every
foxhole filled with water. Thompson sub machine-guns jammed with
the gritty mud and were unreliable in the humid atmosphere."

From General Hanford MacNider in his Foreword to <u>Bushmasters</u> by Roy Lancaster:

"...No attempt has been made to recount the individual exploits of the dozens of units and thousands of heroic men who passed through this tough little command, (158th RCT),

nor has any effort been put forth to picture the deadly heartbreaking monotony of life in the fetid dripping jungles of Panama, New Guinea, and its nearby islands, or the Philippines, where a combination of mountains and dense tropical vegetation made a more difficult fighting country than any other south of the equator. Rain, heat, mud, fever, more rain- month after month, for many of these men year after year- bursts of fierce fighting, long dreary periods of continuous back-breaking labor- no furloughs, no diversions, no anything but more of the same. This constituted the life of the foot slogging Bushmasters."

HEADQUARTERS, 158TH REGIMENTAL COMBAT TEAM

8 October 1945

In relinquishing command of the "Fightingest Little Army" in the American Forces of the Pacific, I want to put into the record my deep personal appreciation of the services of every member of this Combat Team in and out of battle during the year I have had the high privilege of serving with you.

You have been magnificent. You have met every task and every Jap head on. You have whipped them both in the highest and finest tradition of American Arms. It has been a long hard pull far from home and under vicious conditions, but there never has been a moment (and never will be) when you could not look the whole cockeyed world in the eye and be proud to call yourself a "Bushmaster".

No man who has served in this outfit will ever forget or cease to be grateful to those comrades-in-arms who gave so much to this great team and to their country but whom we leave beneath the white markers or bearing through life the wounds of battle.

Good luck to you in all the days ahead. You deserve the best and I am wishing just that for every one of you.

Hanford MacNider
Brigadier General, U. S. Army

HEADQUARTERS FORTY THIRD INFANTRY DIVISION
Office of the Commanding General

APO 43, c/o Postmaster
San Francisco, Calif.
12 February 1945

Subject: Commendation

To   : Commanding General and all Ranks, 158th Regimental
          Combat Team, APO 70

1. Although the campaign for the Island of Luzon and
the liberation of the Philippines is not yet complete, and there
lay ahead of us many difficult tasks and missions before the war
is won, I wish you to know that I appreciate fully the great
effort you have made in connection with the battles that ensued
after our landing.

2. Your Combat Team, charged initially with advancing
north along the coast and protecting the left flank of the Sixth
Army, came under my operational command on 11 January 1945. In
the days that have followed your unit has experienced some of the
fiercest and bloodiest fighting had, during this campaign. You
have advanced and taken your objectives against stubborn and determined enemy resistance, against strong, well-prepared and con-
cealed positions, almost constantly under direct enemy observa-
tion and artillery fire. The tactical skill that you and your
subordinate commanders have used, the courage and determination
of all ranks, are in line with the best traditions of American
fighting men.

The 147th Field Artillery Battalion has supported
your operation and that of other units attached to you in a superior manner. The supporting elements of the Combat Team have
likewise demonstrated high combat efficiency. Your Infantry,
without whom ground can not be taken and held, have been superb.
They have fully demonstrated that the fighting, marching, shoot-
ing, slugging "doughboy" can always take one more step, fire one
more shot, throw one more hand grenade and deliver one more thrust
with the bayonet to gain their final objectives.

3. It has been a real pleasure to have you under my
command for this period. I predict for you in the future even
greater achievements. It has been a privilege for me and for
every member of this Division to have served with you. For high
qualities of leadership, skillful tactics, intrepid and courageous
conduct on your part and all those who serve with you, I commend
you.

LEONARD F. WING
Major General, U. S. Army
Commanding

Reproduced Hq 158th RCT
14 February 1945

290

DEPARTMENT OF THE ARMY

Lineage and Honors

158th INFANTRY
(Bushmasters)

Organized as the 1st Arizona Volunteer Infantry and mustered into Federal service September - November 1865 by companies (A, B, C, E, F) for one year; mustered out September - November 1866

Reorganized by elements May 1882 - April 1892 as 1st Regiment Infantry, Arizona Militia

(Arizona Militia redesignated 19 March 1891 as Arizona National Guard)

Mustered into Federal service May - June 1916 for service on the Mexican border

Drafted into Federal service 5 August 1917

Reorganized and redesignated 3 October 1917 as 158th Infantry, an element of the 40th Division

Demobilized 3 May 1919 at Camp Kearny, California

Reorganized as 158th Infantry, assigned to the 45th Division, and Federally recognized 12 September 1924 with Headquarters at Phoenix

Inducted into Federal service 16 September 1940 at home stations

Relieved 11 February 1942 from assignment to the 45th Division

Inactivated 17 January 1946 in Japan

Reorganized as 158th Infantry and Federally recognized 18 February 1947 with Headquarters at Tucson

Reorganized 1 March 1959 as 158th Infantry, a parent regiment under the Combat Arms Regimental System, to consist of the 1st and 2d Battle Groups

CAMPAIGN PARTICIPATION CREDIT

Indian Wars
Arizona 1866

World War I
Without inscription

World War II
American Theater without inscription
New Guinea (with arrowhead)
Bismarck Archipelago
Luzon (with arrowhead)

DECORATIONS

Philippine Presidential Unit Citation, Streamer embroidered 17 OCTOBER 1944 TO 4 JULY 1945

Company A (Safford), 2d Battle Group additionally entitled to:

Distinguished Unit Citation, Streamer embroidered LINGAYEN GULF

By Order of the Secretary of the Army:

J. C. LAMBERT
Major General, USA
The Adjutant General

FIGHTING 158th

If you want to hear the story of an army
    and its fate
You should ask some lonely Nipponese
    who met the One Five Eight.
The first ones came from the Desert State
    where they trained and soldiered hard
They were then a peacetime army,
    The Arizona National Guard.
Then came that fateful Sunday
    that chilled the blood of man,
The attack on Pearl Harbor
    from the Island of Japan,
and the call for well trained soldiers
    for this war of hell and hate,
so two thousand men were chosen
    for the fighting One Five Eight
There were Indians, there were Spaniards
    from western desert states,
There were Yankees, there were Rebels
    in the fighting One Five Eight.
No one knows when we are coming;
    no one knows from where we came,
But they have all heard the story
    and the terror of our name.
From the silence of the jungles
    some have heard our battle cry,
Few have lived to hear the story
    "We shall win or we shall die".
Now our home is in the jungle;
    We took our name from a jungle snake,
We, the fearless Bushmasters
    of the fighting One Five Eight.
Now when this war is over
    and Japan has met her fate,
She will beg the humble pardon
    of the fighting One Five Eight.
No, you see we're not commandos;
    nor some mighty Ranger band,
But the best damned fighting unit
    from Uncle Sam's great land.
So, if you see a long machete
    with a snake coiled round the blade
On the shoulder of a soldier,
    he helped earn the fame we made,
You should bow in humble gratitude
    and shake his hand elate,
For he has served his country proud and
    well with the fighting One Five Eight.

...

Editor's note: This poem was copied from PFC TIME, October 1945,
labelled "SPECIAL EMBARKATION EDITION".

292

REFERENCES
Books
Arthur, Anthony (1987) *Bushmasters: Americas Jungle Warriors of World War II.* 1st Edition New York, New York St. Martens Press

Bishop, Chris & McNab, Chris (2006) *Campaigns of World War II Day by Day.* 2nd Edition London, England   Amber Books

Captain Braun, Harold (2005*) Braun's Battling Bastards: The Bushmasters of Company B, 1st Battalion, 158th RCT.* 1st Edition Melbourne, Florida Seabird Publishing.

Davidson, John (2011) *The Pacific War Day by Day.* New York, New York Chartwell Books

Green, Michael (1996) *MacArthur in the Pacific: From the Philippines to the Fall of Japan.* 1st Edition Osceola, Wisconsin Motor Books International

Horner, David PhD. (2005) Chapter 7: General MacArthur's War: The South and Southwest Campaigns 1942-1945. *The Pacific War: from Pearl Harbor to Hiroshima pp.*119-141 Great Britain Osprey Publishing

Lancaster, Roy (1981) *Mobilization of the Bushmasters.* 1st Edition Detroit, Michigan Lancaster Publications

Steinberg, Rafael (1978) *Island Fighting World War II.* 2nd Edition Time/ Life Books

Articles on Websites
Arizona Memory Project *Arizona Bushmasters* retrieved from
www.AZmemory.lib.az.us/cdm4

Duis, Perry (2002) *Chicagoans and World War II* retrieved from
http://www.lib.niu.edu

Paltzer, Seth (2016) The Other Foe: The U.S. Army's Fight against
Malaria in the Pacific Theatre 1942-1945.   Retrieved from
armyhistory.org/the-other-foe

Patrick, Joe (2008) *The Bushmasters: Arizona's Fighting Guardsmen*
World War II Forums retrieved from www.ww2f.com/war-
pacific/158thRCT

The Clearing of Papua. retrieved from
http://history.army.mil/books/wwii/MacArthur %20

The Battle of Wadke Island May 1944. Retrieved from
http://www.historyofwar.org/articles/battles_wadke_island

Carlton. Leah (1942*) Fourth of July* world War II
http://www.history.com/topics/ world-warii/battle-of-new-britain-
rabaul

Firsthand Accounts
Col. Erb, Herb (1989) *Bloody Sunday.* File 1018 Arizona State
University Bushmasters Collection

3rd Portable Surgical Hospital. (1945) Record group 407, World War
II Unit Histories. National Archives and Records Administration

Magazine Articles
Andrade, Dale. (updated 2003) *Luzon 1944-1945*. U.S. Army Center of Military History Brochure

Hemingway, Albert B*ushmasters Sorely Tested* Bushmasters Collection Arizona State University

Sgt. Kramer, Dale (1945) *The Bushmasters.* Yank: The Army Weekly New York, New York Bushmasters Collection Arizona State University

Websites
www.encyclopediaofchicago.com
www.imaginesports.com
www.USpostalhistory.com
www.bushmaster.vibogen.com/history
www.chicagotribune.com/news/ct-perflashwwiichicago

Museums
Fort Tuthill Military History Museum, Flagstaff, Arizona

World War II Museum, New Orleans, Louisiana

Arizona Military Museum, Phoenix, Arizona

Arizona State University Library Bushmaster Collection

Film
"Attack" The Battle for New Britain, U.S War Department

Pacific War in Color, Series, Smithsonian Channel
*Island Hopping
*Striking Distance
*No Surrender
*An Ocean Apart

Made in the USA
Monee, IL
10 September 2020